STARTING A BUSINESS
IN THE COUNTRY

More related titles

Book-keeping and Accounting for the Small Business
How to keep the books and maintain financial control over your business

'Compulsory reading for those starting a new business and for those already in the early stages.' – Manager, National Westminster Bank (Midlands)

The Downshifter's Guide to Relocation
Escape to a simpler, less stressful way of life

'...opens your eyes to the implications of downshifting, and considers the main criteria you can use to judge when the time is right for you.' – NFU Countryside

Preparing a Winning Business Plan
How to win the attention of investors and stakeholders

'This book will not only help you prepare a business plan but will also provide a basic understanding of how to start up a business.' – Working from Home

The Small Business Start-up Workbook
A step-by-step book to starting the business you've dreamed of

'A comprehensive and very practical workbook offering a modern approach to self-employment. ... A *must have* for anyone thinking of setting up their own venture.' – Thames Valley News

How To Books
3 Newtec Place, Magdalen Road,
Oxford OX4 1RE, United Kingdom
email: info@howtobooks.co.uk
http://www.howtobooks.co.uk

The Daily Telegraph

STARTING A BUSINESS
IN THE COUNTRY

Ideas and advice for a better lifestyle

WENDY PASCOE

howtobooks

Published by How To Books Ltd,
3 Newtec Place, Magdalen Road,
Oxford OX4 1RE. United Kingdom.
Tel: (01865) 793806. Fax: (01865) 248780.
email: info@howtobooks.co.uk
http://www.howtobooks.co.uk

British Library Cataloguing in Publication Data
A catalogue record for this book is available from the British Library

Cover design by Baseline Arts Ltd, Oxford
Illustrations by Nicki Averill
Produced for How To Books by Deer Park Productions, Tavistock
Typeset by PDQ Typesetting, Newcastle-under-Lyme, Staffs.
Printed and bound in Great Britain by Cromwell Press, Trowbridge, Wiltshire

NOTE: The material contained in this book is set out in good faith for
general guidance and no liability can be accepted for loss or expense
incurred as a result of relying in particular circumstances on statements
made in the book. The laws and regulations are complex and liable to
change, and readers should check the current position with the relevant
authorities before making personal arrangements.

Contents

Introduction

As every sensible person knows, living in the country means a far more pleasant and civilised way of life. It's where people still talk to their neighbours and where children walk to school on their own and play outside. But at the same time it's not an *Archers*-style idyll, and the basic rules of business still apply. Don't think that just because your target customer may live in sleepy Bridport rather than cutting edge Bethnal Green, they're any less discerning or less prepared to go elsewhere if your product or service isn't good enough.

Starting a business in the country is all about recognising the differences between rural and urban situations, picking the right business to suit your area and not imposing city working practices which just won't work in the countryside. Instead, make those differences work for you, learn a different way of doing things and you're half way there already.

According to the Countryside Agency, there are 5.9 million households in rural England alone, and that means a lot of potential customers out there waiting for you and your trade. So cast off those office shackles, that corporate yoke, and get out there and do some business.

Case Studies

Acknowledgements

Thank you to everyone who helped with the book, in particular Alison Gee, Robert Cowie of Winter Rule for his advice on tax and other financial matters, and Suzanne Woodward for supplying the missing chapter. Thanks also to Roger Greenhalgh, Sean Beer and Deborah Lees of the National Rural Knowledge Exchange, Phil Moore, Julia Wheeler on business plans, and volunteer readers Chris and Sue.

1

Countryside Survival Skills

L iving and working in the countryside is different, and not just because there are fields and cows rather than streets and buses. It's different because it's personal, more intimate, individual characters matter and you can make more of an impact more quickly.

Yes, you can live the countryside dream where the pace of life slows, where there's time to think, to sit back and enjoy the seasons, and to simply get to know your family and friends again. But rural life can also be stimulating and productive, and a hugely rewarding environment to do business in, especially if you're new to it.

While life may not be lived as frenetically as in a large town or city, many people find that just as much gets done. If you've ever lived in a city, you'll know only too well the wasted hours spent commuting or just getting around – traffic jams, a fruitless search for a parking space, or the delayed tubes, trains and buses. And in business, those wasted hours cost you money.

The countryside isn't for everyone. There'll be some who'll miss the noise, the excitement, the adrenalin rush of being at the centre of things. For the rest of us though, it'll do just fine.

YOUR DRIVING FACTOR

Starting up your new business, and perhaps moving to the country if you're not here already, is a big step. You'll be tested in the coming weeks and months, both financially and emotionally. There'll be bleak times when you'll wonder if you made the right decision and whether you've dragged your family unintentionally into something which looks like turning out to be a terrible mistake.

One way to keep your sanity is to identify right at the beginning your motives for going self-employed. And in times of crisis, keep repeating your motivation over and over, like a mantra.

There are plenty of possible driving factors:

- You don't want to work for anyone else.
- You don't want to be answerable to anyone else.
- You want to escape from commuting.
- You want to escape from an office existence.
- You want to escape from routine drudgery.
- You want to escape from office politics.
- You are bored.
- You want to do something you enjoy.
- You want to do something you believe in.
- You don't want your children to grow up in a city.

- You want a better life for you and your family.
- You need a new challenge.
- You want to take responsibility for your life.

RISK TAKING: PRUDENCE TO RECKLESSNESS

You've probably been asked about your attitude to risk before. It's a standard question on many investment products and it's just as relevant here. The fact that you're reading this book and are presumably at least considering throwing it all in and starting again already makes you more of a risk-taker than someone who sits in someone else's office until they're 65.

At an early stage you have to think about how far you're prepared to push it. A lot will depend on your family commitments and whether you're the main breadwinner. If it's just you and the cat then it's easier than if you have a partner and children to support. So:

- Are you the type to risk everything on a dream?

- Are you willing to give it a try for a year or two, knowing you could probably go back if you had to?

- Or are you going to go for something like a rock-solid franchise which won't leave much to chance?

Your attitude to risk will affect almost every business decision you take from this point. It's all about living comfortably with your exposure to it. Some will rise to the challenge and will relish risk, thriving on the challenge. Others will dread it and the uncertainty it brings. You have to decide where you sit on this scale.

ADJUSTING TO DOWNSIZING

This book is not about downsizing: there are plenty of those around already. But we'll mention it in passing because it could be an important factor in your calculations.

A 'downsizer' is shorthand for describing someone who's given up their stressed high-maintenance city lifestyle, and used the money from the sale of their home to finance a move to the country and a more relaxed way of life. People already living in the countryside can downsize too in order to start up a rural business. They could be:

♦ giving up the big house and high-powered job in a county town to move to a woodcutter's cottage in deep countryside

♦ or staying in the same house but resigning from their salaried job to start up their own dream business.

Downsizing comes in many forms but the same decisions will still have to be taken and the same adjustments made if your new business stands any chance of being successful.

Points to consider, regardless of which camp you fall into:

♦ Are you prepared, practically and emotionally, for a big drop in salary?
♦ Are you prepared for the loss of professional status?
♦ Are you and your family prepared for a period of uncertainty?
♦ Are you and your family prepared for a lifestyle change?

If you are currently urbanites:

- Will you miss the larger shops and the greater choices?
- Will you miss the nightlife, the clubs and restaurants?
- Will you miss the museums, galleries and exhibitions?
- Will you miss that feeling of being at the centre of events?

And a few practical points to think about:

- Will your family need a second or even third car?
- Are you prepared to taxi your children around the countryside until they can drive themselves?
- What about new schools?
- What about childcare provision?

Case study: The Dorset charcoal producer

Jim Bettle produces and markets English barbeque charcoal. From his base at Sturminster Newton in Dorset, he works with an independent forester who clears and manages small areas of woodland on behalf of the owners. Jim takes the cleared wood, the ultimate natural byproduct, turns it into charcoal, and in doing so produces a better and more effective fuel.

How did you start?

I'd been working on landscape construction and was seeing wood wasted, just burnt to get rid of it. So in 1996 I started the Dorset Charcoal Company. I learnt how to do it by going around the country and watching the old boys. You use a slow cooking process which basically chars the wood and turns it into charcoal.

Who are your customers?

Garage forecourts, garden centres, camp sites and high quality butchers. The charcoal is mostly for barbeques, but I supply some artists' charcoal too.

Is it a good business?

I make a living from it. I have a family to support, but it's a quality of life job. I have one full-time helper and two more seasonal people. Summer is the busiest time. I'm 36 now and I'll continue while my health is good, until my back gives out, because there's a lot of lugging the wood around.

Could anyone do this?

Anyone can make charcoal: the trick is selling it. I've now got the marketing sorted. I believe in the sustainability of it. That's what drives you in the first five years when you're not making any money and living hand to mouth. But the business has gone to plan and it now grows organically.

Dorset Charcoal Company
tel: 01258 818176
website: www.dorsetcharcoal.co.uk
email: inquiries:dorsetcharcoal.co.uk

SKILLS YOU'RE GOING TO NEED

There's a big danger when setting up your own business of too much self-analysis and too much list making. One school of thought says you're better off doing some basic research and then trusting to instinct. The other school says you can never do too much. For those of you in the second camp, here's a way of combining self-analysis and list making.

It's called a SWOT analysis, which is an acronym for Strengths, Weaknesses, Opportunities and Threats. As with most of these things, it won't tell you anything you don't know about yourself already, but it should help focus the mind and show the weak spots which may need a bit of work.

The idea is to draw up a list, identifying your strengths and weaknesses and so on, and then sit back and contemplate the findings. It will help if you discuss the list with someone whose opinion is generally sound.

There are some skills you're going to need to have, and if your analysis shows you're lacking in these areas then you need to think about how to address that.

Flexibility – or thinking sideways

You'll be taking all the decisions in your new business, everything from deciding on the stationery design to the position of the new loos or how long a property lease to sign. You're breaking new ground and there'll be no corporate manual to follow or experienced manager to consult. So you'll need a flexible approach to help you:

◆ Overcome those early hurdles that will inevitably crop up. Thinking around a problem is something that you're going to have to get used to.

◆ Take the wide view and come up with the best business opportunity for you and your circumstances. It may not always be the most obvious one.

◆ Respond to the needs and expectations of your first customers. Your service or product may need tweaking, and in the early days of your business you should be listening and learning. You can't afford to stick rigidly to Plan A if it's not working.

◆ Sit down after a few months and decide if your business is going in the right direction, and if not then why not. That could be the time for brave decisions.

◆ Change direction completely if necessary. You may decide after a year or two that you made the wrong career choice and that becoming self-employed was not for you after all.

But at the same time you can't be too flexible, changing your aims as often as your socks. The trick is to realise when something really isn't working and then act.

Motivation

Another key skill. There's little point going into business if you find it difficult to get out of bed in the mornings.

That doesn't mean that all successful businesses have to run on a strict Monday-to-Friday, nine-to-five timetable. You have to be able to put in the hours because you want to. Plenty of creative people have periods of intense activity and can then sit back and rest and recharge batteries for weeks or months until the next time.

It's all a question of recognising when your busiest times are likely to be and then being prepared to really go for it. Gardeners can take it easy in the winter ahead of a busy and intense spring. Soft furnishers or potters may have to gear their entire working year to the busy pre-Christmas period when most gifts are bought. Writers or illustrators will be at the mercy of their contract deadlines, while carpenters or cabinet makers could be hard at it all year around.

Determination

You've got a terrible cold, the children hate the countryside, you haven't made a sale for a week and the mortgage goes out tomorrow. What are you going to do? Bury your head in your hands and sob or get off your backside and make a sale? It's as simple as that really because you're going to need determination and spades of it.

Fortitude

Even if you live like a saint and do business like Richard Branson, there will still be times when your patience is tested. Goods will not be delivered, the casual workers you'd been depending on to help out in your market garden won't turn up, or it'll rain for three weeks when you desperately need it to be dry in order to finish a big gardening contract.

In these cases you will need fortitude and a lot of it. Previous high-earners who've downsized to the country will be tempted to throw money at the problem. For all the above scenarios that won't work. Others may get stressed or angry to the point where they can't function. Again, not very productive. You'll just have to learn to grit your teeth and accept whatever comes with good grace.

Resourcefulness

Whatever your business, you'll need a degree of practical resourcefulness. In large towns and cities there's an expert on hand, virtually around the clock, to cover most eventualities. In the countryside, especially in the remoter areas, that doesn't happen. So what do you do on a cold winter's night when the power goes and your glasshouses full of tender seedlings are left unprotected? Or your delivery van has developed what you suspect is a minor fault (needs more oil) and the local garage wants to take it in for full surgery? The practical side of small business life needs just as much thought as the artistic or creative side.

Patience

If you live in a city you're probably rolling your eyes, but if you already live in the countryside then you'll know the value of patience. Demanding instant service just doesn't work in the country and will probably have a counter-effect. When a deliveryman turns up, spare a moment or two to chat. Take time to talk to the customers in your shop or studio or the clients of your garden design service. Human contact and the human touch generally means good PR.

Getting to know people

Who you know is important in rural areas. This is not because of any desperate social-climbing or networking reasons but because it's how business is done here. It's how you hear about potential new customers, reliable part-time staff or the best source of quality feed for your livery stables.

Don't assume that you can source everything you need from the internet, *Yellow Pages* or local paper ads because a vast amount of business is conducted via word of mouth, and if you live and work in isolation then you'll be out of the loop.

Your own reputation

Reputations stick. If you become known as the man or woman who's slow to pay their bills it'll take you years to live it down. It's far better to get it right from the beginning, and be seen to be honest, hard-working and someone who's providing a good quality service or product and value for money.

On the whole, if you decide you are going to adopt sharper business practices, it's probably best to start them off on other incomers rather than on someone whose family have been living in the community for generations and who's a cousin to half the village.

Trust

This is what you should be aiming for. Customers should trust you and they should trust your product or skill. If there is no trust, you won't have a business.

Asking nicely

Odd, isn't it, how we forget the basics? Ask nicely for something in the inner cities and you'll get a suspicious look and the assumption that you want something for nothing. Even saying good morning in a shop marks you down as a weirdo. Ask nicely in the country and the chances are that you'll get a friendly, prompt and professional service.

YOUR HEALTH

For most people going into business it's going to have to be perfect, unless perhaps you've got a pre-existing condition and know you can deal with it. A new business requires energy, determination, concentration, vigour and plenty of physical stamina. Being self-employed means that you have to turn up day after day, even if you're feeling terrible, because no work generally means no pay.

THE DOWNSIDE OF COUNTRY LIFE

Living in the country and working for yourself isn't always heaven on earth.

- The business risk is all yours.
- It can get lonely.
- There'll be long hours and hard work.
- The business may fail.
- You may not make enough money to meet your needs.
- You may find it more difficult than you thought to motivate yourself.
- You may discover that you don't like working on your own.

Isolation and loneliness are two of the more common complaints of working life in the countryside, especially if your new trade means you're not likely to meet many people. If you're a smallholder who doesn't sell directly to the public, or perhaps a crafts worker tucked away in a studio, you could go for days or weeks without seeing anyone.

It's important to realise that you're not alone. There are literally millions of others sharing your existence, your experiences and probably a lot of the same doubts and fears. If you think isolation could be a problem for you, then you need to address this right at the beginning. Develop your own support networks. Find other people in similar jobs and introduce yourself. Keep in touch with them. Meet the neighbours. Make time for a social life. All this is even more important if you live alone.

The weather

A strangely high proportion of rural businesses are affected by the weather, and it's not just the obvious ones like farming and gardening.

Isolated areas of the country are more vulnerable to extremes of weather. Roads are blocked by snow, high winds bring down power and telephone lines and flooding can take out acres of land. It's rare for a weather-related problem to last more than a few days, but if your business is likely to operate on tight margins, and you're completely dependent on being able to send out goods 365 days a year or being able to move around freely yourself, then it is something else to consider.

Hostility to outsiders

Some remoter regions of the country can be famously unwelcoming to incomers. 'You're not one of us until you have both sets of grandparents buried in the local churchyard' is a familiar chant. It's probably not personal. If you're unlucky enough to be in this position there probably isn't much you can do apart from staying polite and pleasant and hoping that most people will come around eventually. Don't keep apologising for being born in Dorking because it isn't going to change anything.

If it looks like being a permanent problem which could seriously hinder your business you have to ask yourself if you made the right decision to move there in the first place. Is it time to cut your losses and try elsewhere?

The nosiness factor

Unlike in most cities, you'll almost certainly know your countryside neighbours and have a lot to do with them. Living in a community is, after all, one of the reasons why people move to the country in the first place.

It's a myth that rural dwellers spend their days leaning on farm gates, chewing straw and chatting over village business. In practice everyone is working just as hard as you hope to be and getting on with their own lives.

When you move into an area there will inevitably be interest, especially if you plan on doing something unusual, you've come from somewhere very different (the Bronx) or your lifestyle isn't typical for the area. You're going to have to decide what you're comfortable with and at the same time remember that polite inquiry isn't the same as spying. If you find it too intrusive, it's still possible to move to really remote countryside and buy a property that is so cut-off that you never see your neighbours at all.

YOUR FAMILY

So far this chapter has been all about you. But the step you are taking is likely to have just as seismic effect on your family as it is on you:

- **Financial**. The first and most obvious effect it could have on them. Are you the main breadwinner? Are they going to starve or be forced to go shoeless if you fail?

- **Emotional**. Even the most placid will be under a lot of strain at the start of a new business. If you're more highly strung and prone to mood swings it will be far worse. Is your family prepared for this?

- **Practical**. You will be busy, at least for the first few months. Is your family prepared and able to pick up your share of the household chores?

- **Family time**. Is your family prepared to sacrifice family life and time together, at least until the business is established?

In short, are they behind you 100 per cent?

An obvious way around many of the problems is to try to involve your family in your business as much as possible. Clearly some businesses are more family-friendly than others. Tree surgery, knife sharpening or mountaineering instruction aren't really geared to getting the two-year-old involved, but there are plenty of other lines of work that are. Smiley, polite children, for example, work wonders when trying to attract customers to your craft fair or farmers' market stall. So try to think of positive areas where they can help.

YOUR FRIENDS

In this thinking-of-others section, you may also want to consider the impact your new business could have on your friends.

Good friends are invaluable for general moral support and comfort, helping spread the word and bouncing around ideas. But if you want to keep their friendship:

◆ Don't drone on and on about your business. Stop before their eyes glaze over and they start avoiding you.

◆ Don't borrow money from them unless it's a formal business agreement and both parties are comfortable with the deal.

◆ Don't try to use them as free labour (shop assistant, delivery driver, phone answerer).

◆ Don't try to force them into being your sales rep.

◆ Do try to make time for them and your friendship. Keep doing whatever it is you used to do with them.

2

The Right Job

For many, the most difficult issue of all is finding the right job. Some lucky people with an existing skill, hobby or interest can capitalise on that and step seamlessly into their new life. For the rest of us, it'll probably mean a lot of soul-searching and nights spent staring into the bottom of a wine glass. And that's before you've even started on the practical side. 'How much money am I going to need? Where are we all going to live? And how long can we survive before I start making a profit?'

NARROWING DOWN YOUR OPTIONS

If you really haven't a clue where to start and you only know that you have to get out of whatever it is you're doing at the moment, then there are some basic questions to ask yourself.

First, decide what your endgame is, your ultimate aim.

Hobby job

You may decide you only need a part-time job to bring in a bit of extra spending money. You may even be lucky enough to be able to do something because you enjoy it and any money coming in would be a bonus. But you'd still like to maximise your opportunities.

The breadwinner

You may have a family to support, a mortgage to pay, and your new job has to be a success virtually from the beginning. Much will depend on whether you can change careers and stay in your own home or whether you're downsizing from a city lifestyle and planning on relocating the entire family.

Global domination

Or you could have bigger ambitions still. Perhaps you're so confident in your idea that you want to lay down the foundations of a large business that you can nurture, grow and one day sell on as a going concern. This is playing the long game.

THAT EUREKA MOMENT

The very good news is that you don't need one. Not everyone can invent the internal combustion engine, internet or even the clockwork radio. Millions still make a very good living out of doing something that lots of other people already do. It's just a question of spotting a tiny little niche that you can carve out for yourself.

+ It could be a new product.
+ It could be an existing product with a new twist.
+ It could be a new way of selling it.
+ Or you could be selling it in a place where it isn't available at the moment.

- You could re-brand or re-package something.
- Or perhaps offer it cheaper than anyone else.
- Maybe you can combine two existing products and come up with a brand new one.
- Maybe it's a new manufacturing process.
- Or a new creative process.
- Perhaps using different materials.

The variations and twists are endless.

Try applying the above points to whatever is in front of you now. Say the kitchen table. People have been selling kitchen tables, or at least making them, for hundreds of years. It's one of our most humdrum possessions. Yet a few people are still out there, producing them and presumably making a good living from them. And all those people did was to pick an everyday object, do something slightly different to it and sell it on to a waiting public.

Case study: The Kent horticulturist

Alan Bicker gave up lecturing in social anthropology at the University of Kent to return to his horticultural roots when he started the Garden Fruit Tree Company in 2002. Alan, who lives near Canterbury, raises trained fruit trees and grapevines for the wholesale trade. His customers are garden centres, plant centres and landscapers.

Where did you get the idea from?

I made an exhaustive survey of the commercial fruit growing industry and the burgeoning 'garden' trade. I discounted elements that are already over-supplied and identified 'trained trees' as a niche market.

How important was it for you to start your own business?

At the end of an academic career I was looking for something that would provide a good income in an industry I knew well and I would enjoy doing.

How did you get started?

Before lecturing I'd worked in various aspects of agriculture and horticulture. To date it has cost £55,000 to get the company going. I rented land and buildings that suit the nursery business.

What's been your biggest mistake?

Budgeting. However carefully you budget, it always costs more than you expect. Multiply everything by two and you'll be about right.

And your best move?

Doing it.

What advice would you have for others starting up their own business?

It's not the plan but the planning, so pay attention to detail. Ask advice from everyone you can in the trade you're considering and then make up your own mind. Get a good accounting system: *MYOB* is excellent. *Carpe diem* (seize the day).

WHAT CAN YOU DO?

This is the bit where it's difficult not to sound like a school careers adviser, but if you don't have a clear idea of what to do then you have to sit down and either consider your SWOT analysis or start a fresh list of options.

You could pay to see a private careers adviser. There are many out there, but serious and tailored one-to-one advice over a period of time can be expensive, running into many hundreds of pounds. It's probably better in the first instance to see what you can come up with yourself, using the internet, book shops and the local library, before resorting to professional advice.

But before you do anything, ruthlessly condense into no more than three short sentences:

- ◆ What you can already do.
- ◆ What you're good at.
- ◆ What you really want to do.

This does focus the mind and forces you to think of the realistic options open to you. Aim to end up with something like: 'I'm an accountant. But I know I'm good at teaching. I really want to spend my life sailing so I'll start a sailing school.'

Before you can get to your three short sentences you need to take a long hard look at your life so far.

Qualifications

What did you train as originally? Did you take an agricultural science degree, train as a nursery nurse or study homeopathic medicine? It doesn't matter how far back it goes because it'll still be relevant. You may not be up to speed on the latest developments but you'll still have more experience and knowledge than someone who didn't do it at all.

Have you re-trained in anything? Added another skill to your existing qualifications? You may have had some IT-related training or perhaps followed a managerial or people-management course.

Experience
Go back as far as those teenage jobs. Did you ever pick potatoes, help with the hay-making or look after the neighbours' chickens when they were away? If you were a city child, did you work as a waiter or waitress, behind the bar somewhere or in a shop in the pre-Christmas rush? Where have you travelled? Are you familiar with other cultures? Can you speak another language?

Practical skills
Can you work in wood or metal, sew, cook, paint, design? Do you know your cotoneaster from your cornus? Recognise a beech or a sycamore? Identify small animal tracks or wild flowers? Can you sail, navigate, interpret a chart? The skills you've picked up while following your hobby could now be just as important as any academic or professional qualifications you used in your previous 'proper' job.

Personal strengths
Perhaps you're creative with a good eye for colour, or maybe organisation and attention to detail is more you. Do you have a strong social sense or vocation? Are you a carer? Have you drive, vision, focus? Are you good at motivating people? Can you motivate yourself?

Personal weaknesses

Maybe money and figures aren't your strong point. Perhaps you're slow at getting started. Or are you short-tempered and impatient? Do you panic or worry easily? Do you not get on with people as well as you think you should? Do you sometimes feel misunderstood?

Hobbies/interests

What is it you really like doing? Is it walking by the sea or up mountains or just being outside? Are you never happier than when you're pottering around the kitchen or in a workshop or studio? Do you prefer curling up with a good book? Are you most comfortable being around children all day?

What next?

At the end of the exercise get someone who knows you well, whose opinions you trust and who you know will be honest, to look over your conclusions. They may well pick up on something you've missed because it's too obvious. And another person's view is always useful anyway.

Don't be downhearted about the weaknesses. They're not a problem as long as you do something about them. If you're terrible with figures then find a business partner who isn't. If you shy away from people then sell through a shop or agent. If you're disorganised set yourself daily targets of tasks to achieve.

CAREER OR PSYCHOMETRIC TESTING

If you want to take a more structured, less DIY approach then think about career or personality tests, also known as psychometric testing.

There are dozens of variations but essentially they all do the same thing. By you providing a series of answers, solutions or responses to questions or scenarios, you reveal your strengths, weaknesses, likes, dislikes and so on. And in that way, you're led to groups of jobs or professions which would most suit you.

Most tests essentially explore the same areas:

- ability
- aptitude
- personality.

They also explore your personal values and ask you to rate or grade what's important to you, for example:

- lifestyle
- power
- status
- social or altruistic motives
- security
- achievement.

If you think testing could be helpful, start off by having a look on the internet. Worldwide, there are 2.5 million matches for the words 'career tests' and a third of a million in the UK alone, so there should be something out there to suit you. Some sites offer completely free testing, others offer initial or preliminary free testing with the option of buying a more detailed analysis later. With others you pay up front.

The good ones do work, not necessarily because they come up with any startling revelations, but because they help crystallize your abilities, narrow your options and point you in a realistic direction.

Don't expect a big shining light to appear as you finish the last page: 'The job for you is (pause) ... Lion Tamer!' Instead, a good test may conclude you're strong on organisation, logic and people skills and therefore should consider a career in management. Or you may emerge as a largely creative person who works best under little pressure, who needs some support and has no strong financial motive, and therefore is best working in an arts co-operative.

THE JOB
Having established the answers to your three short questions, now turn your attention to the specifics. The following isn't a definitive list: instead use it as a prompt to get you thinking for yourself.

Accommodation provider
Requirements: good people skills, physical fitness, practical aptitude, suitable house/land, access to finance, good business head.

Bed and breakfast
Camping/caravanning site
Guesthouse
Hostel
Hotel, country house
Hotel, town or village
Self-catering cottage

Animals, pets
Requirements: likes animals, possible access to finance, possible premises.

Breeding
Cattery
Dog training

Dog walking
Kennels
Pet cemetery
Pet grooming
Pet hotel
Pet sitting
Stables/livery stables

Antiques
Requirements: knowledge of antiques, good research skills, possible large premises, possible access to start-up finance.

Antique dealer
Antiques restoration
Auctioneer/auction house employee
Clock/watch restorer
Picture framer
Picture restorer

Artists, craftspeople
Requirements: good with hands, design-orientated, probable patience, a workshop or studio.

Artist (general)
Artist (portraits: people)
Artist (portraits: pets)
Candle maker
Ceramicist
Glass/stained glass worker
Interior designer (rustic/contemporary)
Jeweller
Leather goods worker

Potter
Sculptor
Tile maker/designer

Design – IT and traditional

Requirements: possible formal training, contacts, software, raw materials.

Books, brochures, leaflets
Ceramics
Clothes
Corporate design
Fabrics
Graphics
Illustration
Logos
Shoes

Food and drink/retail

Requirements: knowledge of food industry regulations (hygiene, health and safety), good people skills, likes food, imaginative, access to finance.

Baker
Café (organic, vegetarian, vegan)
Caterer/supplier to self-catered cottages
Cheesemaker/dairy products producer
Cheese shop
Chef
Confectioner
Deli
Dinner party catering

Home producer: jams, chutneys, relishes, pickles
Inn/pub
Mobile deli (bike, van, horseback!)
Mobile groceries round
Organic box scheme
Party organiser
Patissier
Picnic/hamper supplier
Restaurant (fish, local produce, game)
Special occasion cakes
Sweet shop
Tea room
Wine bar
Wine importer
Wine merchant
Yacht catering (day or passage)

Environment
Requirements: a believer, contacts, some relevant formal training an advantage.

Alternative energy consultant (wind, waves, tidal, geothermal)
Campaigner
Lobbyist

Gardens, agriculture
Requirement: able to work outdoors all year, physically fit, possible access to finance, some formal training an advantage.

Bulb specialist
Farm
Garden centre

Garden design
Garden furniture design
Garden maintenance
Hanging baskets supplier
Landscape gardening
Market garden
Nursery
Orchard
Smallholding
Trout fishery, fish farm
Vineyard

IT
Requirements: IT skills, knowledge of business environment.

Computer/IT troubleshooting
Desktop publishing
Small company IT consultant
Website design

Natural therapists
Requirements: relevant training, interest in health and complementary health treatments, good people skills.

Acupuncture
Alexander Technique
Aromatherapy
Homeopathy
Hypnotherapy
Osteopathy
Pilates
Reflexology

Reiki
Shiatsu
Therapeutic counselling

Needlework/fabric skills
Requirements: good tailoring skills, eye for colour and texture, professional-standard equipment, meticulousness.

Curtain maker
Designer (clothes, fashion)
Embroiderer
Fabric/textile designer
Knitter/crocheter
Maker of accessories
Milliner
Seamstress/tailor
Soft furnisher (cushions, throws, wraps)
Upholsterer

Retail, non-food
Requirements: business acumen, access to finance, good at trend-spotting.

Accessories, shop or direct sales
Baby, children's clothes
Book shop
Clothes hire
Clothes shop
Evening wear hire
Fancy dress hire
Farm shop
Florist

Gallery
Gift shop
Hats
Niche clothes
Second-hand designer clothes
Shoes
Soft furnishings/household
Vintage clothes/accessories

Rural trades

Requirements: knowledge of the trade, probable physical strength, ability to problem solve, prepared to work in harsh conditions.

Blacksmith
Coppicer
Dry stone waller
Farrier
Firewood supplier
Hedge layer
Installer/restorer of ranges and woodstoves
Metal worker
Stone mason
Thatcher
Wood carver

Tourism, leisure

Requirements: probable relevant formal teaching qualification, knowledge of relevant health and safety legislation, good people skills.

Abseiling instructor
Balloonist
Climbing instructor

Cycle hire
Guided walking, riding, cycling
Local history tours
Orienteering instructor
Party/event organiser, children
Party/event organiser, adults
Riding instructor
Ski/snowboard instructor (Scotland!)
Specialist holidays (walking, horse riding, conservation)

Water-based
Requirements: possible formal teaching or other relevant qualification, possible access to finance, probable good people skills.

Angling supplier
Beach lifeguard
Boat builder/repairer
Boat charter
Diving instructor (deep sea, scuba)
Fisherman
Sailing instructor
Sail maker
Surfing instructor
Windsurfing instructor
Yacht delivery

Woodworking
Requirements: good with hands, meticulousness, eye for design, problem-solving skills, possible premises.

Carpenter/joiner
Exterior windows, shutters and doors designer/builder

Furniture/cabinet maker
Garden furniture designer/builder
Garden shed designer/builder
Picture framer
Traditional toy maker
Tree house designer/builder

Other
Child care
Franchise holder (see Chapter 7)
Local author
Photographer (book/magazine illustration, landscape, portraits, wildlife)
Private tuition (music, languages, English and maths)
Writer

DO YOU HAVE THE PASSION?

Let's assume that you've found the job that you want to do. Now ask yourself if you believe in it completely. Are you passionate about it? Are you prepared to give it total commitment? Consider:

◆ If you're not passionate about your idea, how can you expect anyone else to be?

◆ If you're lukewarm about it now, how are you going to feel in six months or a year's time when you've worked continuously on your project and thought about nothing else?

There's no substitute for really wanting to do something, and it should shine through.

DO YOU HAVE THE USP?

Your USP is your Unique Selling Point. You've come up with your job idea but what's going to make you different, stand out from the crowd? Essentially it means: what's your new twist? Perhaps you've re-invented that kitchen table so that it dangles from the ceiling (no legs so easier to clean underneath), or have come up with a fabulous new combination of flavours for a chutney or relish.

You need a USP because:

- It gives you something to focus your promotions and marketing on.

- It answers people who say: 'Why you and why your product or service?'

LOCATION, LOCATION...

Despite the internet, some jobs and services still don't travel. You need to ask yourself if your new job is right for the place where you're going to be living.

- Will your product or service be affordable locally? Are you in an economically well-off area where there's going to be a demand for a high value childcare service or handmade shoes? Remember that many of the peripheral regions of the country aren't as prosperous as the south east.

- If your job is outdoors, is it weather or climate dependent? If you're a stone waller in the north east of Scotland, how much work will you do in the winter when there are limited daylight hours?

- If you're a tree surgeon, don't move to a tree-less Scottish island. If you want to grow early potatoes or January daffodils, don't move to the Lake District.

- Will your business be dependent on people and crowds? Again, don't move to that Scottish island.

- If you're a potter or artist, do you really want to move to the Cornish resort of St Ives where there's so much existing competition?

COMMON MISTAKES TO AVOID

By now you should be virtually there in deciding what you want to do, where and how. It's easy at this stage to get carried away by enthusiasm and massively underestimate the scale of the task ahead. So:

- Make sure you give yourself plenty of time to do all the preparation, research and finance raising before committing yourself to a launch date. Don't think you'll be ready by a fortnight Tuesday because you won't be. Think months rather than weeks.

- Don't skimp on the time it'll take you at the beginning to work out your costs. Being under-funded can kill you off before you start.

- Make sure you always focus on what the customer wants and not what you think they want.

- Make sure you have all the necessary skills for your new life.

3

Your Market Research

Y ou personally may be absolutely sure there's a demand for your pots of home-dried herbs or landscape photographs, but it's far less risky if you do some market research first.

The main points to establish are:

- if there's a demand for your product or service
- who your customers are likely to be
- where they live and currently shop
- how much money they're prepared to spend
- when they're likely to spend it
- how far they'll travel to find you or whether you'll have to go to them.

There are plenty of ways of carrying out your market research. It all depends on what type of business you're going into and how much work you're prepared to put in.

Options include:

- questionnaires or interviews with target clients – offer inducements/bribes for people to return questionnaires
- street vox pops
- visiting competitors' shops or studios and sampling their product or service
- reading competitors' websites and sales brochures
- doing internet searches for unknown rivals
- doing internet searches for the latest news in your field
- reading the relevant specialist magazines
- questioning people at relevant trade shows and demonstrations
- conducting telephone surveys. These are difficult to do and the findings can be uncertain so only bother doing them if you have a list of contact names and numbers of people who've at least expressed an interest in your business in the past.

THE ART OF QUESTIONING

A lot of our market research will be about asking questions. How you ask is important because you need both co-operation and honest answers. If you start politely and pleasantly most people are happy to help as long as they know you're not selling anything (not yet anyway). Unfortunately many people will tell you what they think you want to hear rather than what they really think. Make sure you frame your questions in such a way that this is less likely to happen. This means asking open questions, along the lines of:

'How much are you prepared to spend on a case of wine/hand-built kitchen/dog walking service?'

Rather than a leading question:

'Would you agree that £90 for a case of New Zealand sauvignon blanc is a reasonable price?'

HOW TO STOP PEOPLE ON THE STREET

Stopping complete strangers on the street and asking them questions is an art. The first couple of times will be terrifying. But when your confidence begins to build and you relax you'll start to enjoy it.

The trick to getting their co-operation is to explain briefly that you're starting up a new business and wondered if they could spare a couple of minutes to help you with your research. Few people will refuse a direct appeal unless they're in a tearing hurry.

When to do it

◆ Don't do surveys in the rain, cold or wind. People won't stop and talk. Instead, hope for a balmy sunny day when people are more likely to linger.

◆ Don't do surveys at the very beginning of the day. Most people on the streets then are in a hurry to get to work.

◆ Don't do surveys at the end of the day. People are tired and want to go home.

Where to do it

◆ Find a place where passers-by naturally slow down (successful hitchhikers use the same technique). This could be near a particularly good window display, under a large shop awning or in a traffic-free mews where it's easier to linger. Slow them down even more by approaching them and making eye contact. But don't get too close: you want their help, not frighten their children.

◆ People sitting on park benches or walls are an even easier target. They're sitting down so they're not in a hurry, and they won't bother to get up and move unless they think you're weird.

◆ Don't go to places where people will be in a hurry. That means bus and railway stations at commuting time, car parks and outside supermarkets (all that frozen food defrosting).

◆ But outside commuting times, bus and railway stations are good because passengers are bored with waiting and happy to be distracted. You may get thrown off if you don't ask permission from the authorities first, but they're not going to lock you up. You get a good cross section of people to ask, especially at large mainline railway stations.

◆ Don't stand outside schools unless it's relevant to your business (you want to question parents about your new line in toddler clothing) and you've spoken to the head teacher first.

◆ Don't do surveys in shops or on their doorsteps unless you've cleared it with them first otherwise they'll throw you out. If you do want to go inside, then try to pick independent stores where there'll be one boss who can say yes or no immediately. It's impossible to get a straight answer from chain stores and you'll spend a day being passed from department to department until you find someone 'authorised' to make a decision.

◆ But do try harder for a relevant shop. A provider of tailored walking or cycling holidays should try to catch customers at an outdoor/leisure store. Enlist the help of that shop. It's in their interests: more people cycling or walking or doing outdoor things ultimately means more customers buying their products.

Other tips
◆ Target big groups. That way you get a lot interviews done but only have to give one initial explanation.

- Dress sensibly and non-threateningly. You may be a fine artist or sculptor who rarely changes out of paint- or clay-splattered overalls. OK in a studio but not if you're intercepting potential customers on the street.

- Clipboards are useful but many potential interviewees will back into the nearest shop at the first sign of one. Compromise by keeping a hard-backed notebook in your bag and whip it out when you've got someone to talk to.

WHAT TO ASK

Don't ask lots of questions. The answers to a few carefully thought out questions will be far more valuable. If you've been droning on, you'll just get short and rushed answers that people only give in order to get rid of you. Get through the questions quickly and professionally. If you spend five minutes talking about the weather with each interviewee you'll be there for weeks.

The type of specific and open questions you should ask:

- You're opening a vintage dress shop/fish restaurant/garden design service. Would the interviewee ever consider using it?

- If so, how much would they be likely to spend?

- How often?

- How far would they travel to buy a dress/eat a meal/commission a new garden?

- Would they use a more expensive personalised service? Dresses/meals/garden designs delivered to their homes?

- Do they already use an existing vintage shop/fish restaurant/garden design service?

◆ If so, which one?

◆ If the interviewee is not interested in what you're offering, why not?

◆ Is the price too high?

◆ Or is what you're offering not quite right?

◆ If so, what could you do to persuade them to change their mind?

You may also want to prepare a list of supplementary questions that you could ask if the interviewee is really keen.

YOUR TARGET CUSTOMER

So you know what, where, when and how to ask questions. All you have to do now is identify your target customer. This is one of the foundation stones of market research. There is absolutely no point in asking a group of elderly ladies about yacht charter or teenagers about their thoughts on hanging baskets. The odd one may be interested because it would make a good birthday present for his mum. But don't waste your time: you're far better off concentrating your efforts on people who are likely to be typical customers.

So before you take to the streets, decide on:

◆ the likely age of your target customer
◆ their sex
◆ social background
◆ possible profession
◆ where they live
◆ if they have children
◆ what their hobbies are.

Some of this is going to be guesswork until you get talking to people, but you can tell a surprising amount from how people are dressed, where they're shopping and who they're with. This isn't pre-judging: it's using common sense.

There's no minimum number of people to talk to, but it has to be enough to give a decent range of answers. Ten people are too few: a thousand isn't practical unless you're prepared to spend months doing it. Perhaps aim to speak to, or receive completed questionnaires from, between 20 and 80 people. Remember that you can use family and friends too if they're relevant. That should be more than enough to see patterns beginning to emerge.

At the end of the surveys, sit down and collate your findings. Remember that it's not a book that you're writing, but just a few notes which are largely for your benefit. Aim to end up with a summary something like:

> *About three quarters of the women I questioned (aged between 30 and 60) said they'd be interested in buying vintage dresses. The maximum they'd be prepared to spend was £200. Half said they'd be prepared to drive ten miles to my shop, and a quarter said they'd drive up to 20 miles. Eighty per cent of the women said they'd only buy a vintage frock for a special occasion, and that would probably be around Christmas.*

So, on the basis of your research so far you've established that there's definitely a demand there for your shop. You probably need to be in a town at the centre of a good road network. You've established the most your customers are likely to pay. And you've also learnt that the run up to Christmas is likely to be your busiest time, so you need to think about how you can boost trade the rest of the year.

Case study: The Cumbrian meat producers

The Foot and Mouth epidemic of 2001 cost Jane Emerson and Peter Stoeken their entire core breeding stock of deer on their Cumbrian hill farm and forced a change of direction. They decided to concentrate on meat production rather than breeding, and in 2004 started selling venison and beef direct to the customer. They've now built their stock back up to a herd of 400 Red Deer and 40 pedigree Dexter cattle.

Why venison?

It's a healthy, low fat red meat. It's the next big thing. At the moment consumers are unsure because they don't know how to cook it and are worried it could be strong or expensive. So we provide recipes and cooking directions too. We sell direct from the farm, through farm shops, farmers' markets and quality food shops. And we're in organic conversion which should open up new markets.

What's been the response so far?

It's early days but so far it's been quite promising. We're only just starting to see some income and wouldn't expect to make any money this year. We need to do more product development. After venison sausages, burgers, kebabs and the like, maybe cooked meats and things like salami. But that's for the future.

What's your background?

Peter and I worked in forestry and landscape contracting. We employed staff and had business management and contracts experience before we took up farming. We've both drawn on that experience.

Do you have any advice to pass on?

Don't underestimate the time and financial resources you'll need to go into business. If you're on a shoestring, forget it. Things can and will go wrong. You need strength of character to cope. You don't know how difficult things can be until you've made money and then lost it. You have to have a positive frame of mind.

Deer 'n' Dexter
tel: 01768 480069
fax: 01786 483809
website: www.deer-n-dexter.co.uk
email: jane@deer-n-dexter.co.uk

CHECKING ON THE COMPETITION

Market research isn't just about asking questions of potential customers. You should be researching the wider picture too.

Finding out about the competition is key. This is where you can learn a great deal about your business, and it's also quite good fun being a spy. So where is the enemy? How many are out there? Does it matter if you have a rival in the next village? What exactly are they offering? How much do they charge? What are their terms and conditions? Are they any good? How can you be better?

Places to check for competitors:

◆ internet search
◆ local and national phone books
◆ local paper adverts
◆ specialist websites, directories and magazines
◆ specialist clubs and associations
◆ asking around.

Go and visit them, either anonymously or upfront.

Business competitors don't necessarily have to be local to you. If you're setting up as a wine merchant, then Sainsburys or Oddbins is as much a competitor as the wine merchant in the next market town.

At the very minimum level of market research, don't even think about setting your own prices until you know what your competitors are charging.

SUPPLIERS

While you're conducting your market research you can tackle suppliers at the same time. In compiling your supplier's list, try to have two or three alternatives lined up. Never become too dependent on a single supplier in case they let you down.

As with everything, word of mouth is best. Failing that, check the internet and magazines aimed at your type of business, the *Yellow Pages* and other phone directories. Don't be bashful about asking other businesses about their suppliers: they can only say no. But many will take it as a compliment rather than a threat because you are, in a roundabout way, praising them. So if you see a well-fitted deli or accessories shop, find out where they sourced the shelving or who did the design. Or if you admire the quality of tools the landscaper is using in the next-door garden, hop over the wall and ask him where he got them.

Good suppliers are also an invaluable source of market research information because they've probably been in your business for a long time and will have seen a lot of people come and go. Encourage them to chat and tell you all about it.

OTHER RESEARCH

There's plenty of other more general research you can conduct from your desk. Find out about the general state of the business you're going into – catering, tourism, crafts, alternative health, whatever. Look for the trends and check that it's not in terminal decline. What's tipped to be the next development or technique, the next must-have bit of equipment, the next fad?

The internet is the obvious starting point to look. But don't rule out organisations like the high street banks which can be extremely knowledgeable about small businesses local to them, as well as being aware of the more general economic trends. Most have small business advisers. Banks are keen to attract new start-up business accounts (presumably because they hope to make pots of money out of them) and will have a bewildering range of services and products to tempt you. So go along and find out what they can do for you. If they want your account, then make them help you do your homework first. And don't overlook libraries. They still do exist in the age of the internet, and very useful they can be too. Many still have excellent reference sections.

IF YOU'RE REALLY SERIOUS

If you're determined to do some really thorough market research, then there are many organisations out there which follow consumer and economic trends and publish endless reports, statistics and analysis. You'll have to pay for a lot of the good material, and for the majority of people starting out on a small rural business career it won't be worth it.

However, if you do want to try, you could start with an organisation like Mintel which focuses on consumer goods and trends. Its website address is www.mintel.com. Otherwise do an internet search and you'll have ample choice.

ONGOING RESEARCH

Market research doesn't stop dead on your first day of trading: it's a continuing process. Nothing ever stands still, least of all fickle consumer demand. You need constant research in order to anticipate new trends and to make sure you never get left behind.

You don't have to take to the streets every six months armed with a new questionnaire unless you really want to. Instead:

◆ Read all websites, magazines and literature relevant to your business.

◆ Talk to suppliers who'll know what your competitors are up to.

◆ Keep in touch with any trade or specialist association in your field.

Existing clients and customers

The client base is hugely valuable for market research purposes. Your customers have already used your product or service so they'll have a view worth hearing. Also, loyal and regular customers will begin to feel they have a stake in your business, especially if they've been with you from the beginning, and won't hold back if they think you're doing something wrong.

Ask them:

◆ Why were they interested in the first place.
◆ What they think of your product or service now that they've used it a few times.
◆ What they think about the pricing. Too expensive. Value for money.
◆ What they think you could improve on.
◆ What other things they think you should be doing (new lines, new services).

TRADING STANDARDS

At about this stage, while you're thinking in detail about your new product, you may need to speak to your local authority's trading standards department. This is especially relevant if you're making anything that has a safety element or fire risk, such as upholstered goods or clothing. If so, your product will be checked to make sure it meets the appropriate regulations.

Market research can be as basic or as thorough as you want. It's not a school project and you're not going to get lines if you don't do it. But the more research you do, the better chance your business has of succeeding. Ultimately it's all about identifying a gap in the market which you can squeeze your business into.

4

The Business Plan

This isn't negotiable. If you are remotely serious about starting up your own business you are going to have to do one. There's no mystique surrounding a plan; it should be easy and even enjoyable to do, and it won't cost anything except your time.

You need a business plan because:

- It'll show you if there are any serious flaws in your business.
- It'll show you if your business is likely to succeed.
- It'll show you if there's likely to be a market for your product or service.
- It'll show you if you're likely to make any money.
- It'll show you if there's likely to be a future in your business.
- You will not be able to borrow money or apply for grants or loans without one.

- No external funder or adviser will take you seriously without one.
- Your business is more likely to fail without one.

A business plan is also useful because it provides you with a way of measuring the success of your business.

WHAT IS A BUSINESS PLAN?

A business plan is simply a logically laid out document which brings together in the same place all the information and research you've carried out on your business. It should also include details of what your competitors are up to, as well as other outside influences such as an assessment of economic conditions.

An economic assessment may sound daunting, but it's not. It could just be noting that interest rates are at seven per cent and rising, and you know you'll need to borrow £50,000 to open your livery stables. Therefore, as a result of your assessment, you decide to wait until interest rates are down to a more manageable five or six per cent.

Or perhaps you decide unemployment in your area is too high, and wages too low, to support your dream of a small but upmarket florist's shop. Again you may decide to wait or try the town up the road which is more affluent.

WHY IT WORKS

A business plan works because it forces you to consider your business from all angles. This means what the business is, where the money's coming from, if there's a gap in the market and if it's likely to be profitable.

A lot of it is estimated because you'll be anticipating what's likely to happen in the future. But base it on some clear and thorough initial research and you'll be surprised, eventually, at how accurate it turns out to be.

Case study: The North Wales home support providers

Across the rural county of Conwy in North Wales, Darren and Sharron Jones provide care and support to the elderly or those with learning or physical disabilities who want to stay living in their homes. They launched their company, AKC Home Support Services, in 1991 after identifying a gap in the market.

What do you do exactly?

We provide help for all aspects of daily living, from cleaning to cooking. We give support to our clients rather than doing everything for them. For example, someone confined to a wheelchair can still cook: we just make sure they have the tools.

What's your background?

I'd worked in finance and import/export so knew about the management side. Sharron had experience of the care sector. Legislation was changing and care in the community was being introduced. We recognised there was an opportunity and went for it.

Did you do a business plan?

Yes, and we still do. We started on a £40 per week enterprise allowance scheme and needed the business plan to negotiate a business bank account overdraft facility. We do plans as per changing needs, certainly annually and when we need finance. They provide a benchmark to see if you've achieved what you wanted to. We would probably still have been successful without one, but it eased the process. You can still do a job with only half the tools but it'll take you longer.

Do you have any advice?

Don't get sidetracked. Stay focused. Be prepared to bin clients who don't pay. We had one big client who wasn't paying. He told me that I couldn't afford to drop him but I did. The business is bigger than a single client.

WHAT TO PUT IN YOUR PLAN

It's got to be detailed but not long-winded. Most business plans can probably be fitted onto a maximum of about 12 to 15 sheets of A4 paper. Much longer and no one's going to read it, but you can include back-up material as appendices.

There are two main audiences for your business plan:

◆ yourself
◆ a potential financial backer and/or business adviser.

It has to be interesting. If you're bored writing about your business in the plan then you'll be bored doing it. If your funder or backer is bored they won't read your plan and you probably won't get your money.

So the rules when writing it:

◆ Keep it snappy but don't be flippant.
◆ Be precise and detailed but don't go on.
◆ Keep it ordered.

Formats will vary, there's no definitive way of putting together a business plan, but it should probably include the following elements:

Executive summary

Oddly, it's usual for a business plan to start with a summary, known as an executive summary. The idea is that many would-be backers or advisers don't have the time or can't be bothered to read the whole document. They'll read the précis and make a preliminary judgement. If they're interested they'll go on and read the rest, but if they're bored or not impressed with your ideas then they won't go any further.

So it's critical that your executive summary is well-written, informative and covers all the main points of the business plan. Again, there's no set format but it probably shouldn't be much longer than a side of A4. You'll probably find it easier to write the executive summary *after* you've written the main plan.

Mission statement

A mission statement isn't a bit of cheesy American corporate psychobabble but a useful way of reminding yourself, your staff, customers and suppliers what it's all about. It's a direct statement of what you want to achieve and the philosophy behind your business. It shouldn't be any longer than a sentence or phrase.

Microsoft, no less, keeps its mission to the point: 'To enable people and businesses throughout the world to realize (sic) their full potential' ... though it does take a further page to elaborate on its values. Or how about this one from the women's fashion retailer Phase Eight: 'To offer a shopping experience that exceeds expectations and clothes that give pleasure in the buying and wearing.'

Try for yourself, something like:

'Somerset Farmhouse Cheeses: help us spread the word that there's more to cheese than Cheddar.'

Or it can be more literal:

'Joe Bloggs Portrait Photography. We capture your family through every milestone. Studio or at-home portraits available. Pets by arrangement. We have the vision.'

And it's not set in stone: as your business evolves then so should your mission statement. Stick the statement on the wall and re-read it when you're feeling low, think you've lost your sense of direction or need some motivation.

A mission statement isn't compulsory for your business plan, but if you are going to include one then it should be close to the beginning.

Personal or team profile
This is obviously about you and where you sell yourself. Include your CV, emphasising relevant skills, qualifications and experience; an assessment of your strengths and weaknesses; reasons for starting up your own business; and personal hopes and ambitions.

It's important to make this section as strong as possible – though don't overdo it, claiming you conquered Everest at 15. Your business is going to succeed or fail because of you and no one else, and therefore any outside backer is going to be taking a long hard look at what you've got to say.

If you have a business partner or staff already lined up to employ then you also need to sell them. Explain in the plan what they'll bring to your business in terms of skills, experience and perhaps finance. If there's a weakness, perhaps lack of direct sales experience, then this is where you should say what you intend to do about it. It's also important to demonstrate commitment, so say how much time and money you and any partners and staff are putting into the business. If it's important that your business plan helps you secure funding then emphasise any professional advisers you have, including accountants and lawyers.

There's no right or wrong place in the business plan to include the personal or team profile. If the business is about you as an individual and a personality (reflexologist, healer), then give the profile more emphasis and include it towards the beginning of the plan. If your new business is more about the product (luxury organic chocolate truffles), then you may want to drop the profile down to below the sections on market research and sales strategy.

Business opportunity

This is about selling your business, explaining your vision of it and setting out how and why you think it's viable. But again it has to be believable. Don't claim you want 100 branches of your sandwich round to be established before Christmas if you have no experience of food retailing and only £500 start-up money.

The first sentence should be a description of your business, something along the lines of: 'This company will offer personalised walking and horse riding holidays in Yorkshire, sold mostly via its own website.' At most use two sentences. If you can't condense your description into these two sentences your aims are almost certainly too broad. If you aren't clear and concise in your description then your own focus probably isn't any clearer.

Then state:

- The business name.

- An outline of your product or service and who your customers are likely to be.

- When you hope to start trading. Or if you've taken over an existing business, what the history is, how long it's been trading and how you want to develop it.

- An outline of the present market.

- Any gaps in the market.

- What makes your product or service different, the unique selling point (USP).

- Any competitive edge you may have (previous experience, lots of start-up capital, ability to build your own website).

- The objectives of your business and likely timescale, over one, five and ten years (in Year One establish website and sell 30 holidays: by Year Ten have own premises, run 5,000 holidays and employ team of walking guides).

- An assessment of the business's likely strengths and weaknesses. (Strengths include the advantage of not having to build up expensive stocks of a product or raw material; weaknesses include the chance of another Foot and Mouth type incident closing off the countryside.) This is also the point to include your economic assessment.

You may have lived and dreamed of your young business for months, and become immersed in its world, but remember that the readers of your plan almost certainly won't know it like you do. So avoid jargon and don't assume too much prior knowledge, especially if you're going into something obscure (restoring ancient stained glass windows, importing rare seeds). If you're not sure, get a friend or family member who doesn't know the subject to check that it's readable.

Market research

Again, if you want to be taken seriously by an outside backer or adviser, then you have to be seen to be doing proper market research. So here you explain your research methods, the results and then your conclusions.

Be honest. If you put too positive a gloss on things you're only fooling yourself and any experienced outsider reading your plan will see through it anyway.

You may also want to construct one or two 'what-if?' scenarios to show you've thought about other possibilities:

◆ What happens if an existing competitor substantially increases its advertising budget and takes on extra staff?

◆ What happens if another competitor moves into the local area?

◆ What happens if there's a general economic downturn and people start cutting their spending on non-essential goods and services?

Overall in this section you have to demonstrate that you're familiar with the market you're going into, that you understand what drives that market and can recognise any trends which could affect sales.

Advertising, marketing and sales strategy

This stage of the plan follows logically on from the last. Your research has demonstrated that there is a demand for your product or service, so now you have to show how you intend to get it 'to market', as the jargon goes. According to Business Link, the national business advice service set up by the Department of Trade and Industry, this section is often the weak link in business plans, so it's worth putting in the effort to make it right, achievable and credible.

You need to say:

- What your objectives are (you want to make every household within 15 miles aware of your name, you want to reach all working women between 30 and 55 in your local market town).

- What methods of advertising you intend to use.

- How much it's likely to cost.

- How often per year you intend to do it.

- How you're going to set your prices.

- How you intend to sell. This means via a shop, craft fair or farmers' market, on the internet, face-to-face or even on the phone.

The operations
This is about the practicalities of your business, so include:

- Where you're going to work from and how much it's going to cost. Do you have to take on a lease? How much are your insurances?

- How you're going to make your product.

- At what point, if at all, you will employ someone to do the manufacturing while you concentrate on design or developing the product further. (This is relevant regardless of whether you'll be producing pottery, furniture, sticky cakes or hand-stitched shoes.)

◆ How much spare manufacturing capacity you have. Are you able to expand using your available equipment and space or will you need to invest money in larger premises and more equipment in the future?

◆ How you'll deliver a service or skill to your clients, if that's what you're offering. What's the typical length of an appointment and where will you meet? Will clients need aftercare?

◆ Methods of payment and terms of payment. (Cheque with bankers' card/major credit cards/account holders only. No credit/ 30 days' credit/three months' credit.)

◆ Transport. If you need to get around, how are you going to do it?

◆ Distribution. If you have a product, how are you going to get it to your customers? If you're producing two or three large pieces of fine furniture every six months you can afford to arrange special delivery. But if it's something on a larger scale, organic vegetable boxes going weekly to 500 customers across two counties or scented oils distributed to shops throughout the UK, you're going to need a professional and reliable system of delivery.

◆ Your IT system. What equipment and software you'll have, how it'll be used to run your business, what back-ups you'll have in place and the steps you've taken to make sure it's secure.

◆ Your system of management. This means you have to show you have systems in place for stock control, quality control and for doing your accounts. If you do expand, will your systems be able to cope?

If your business is going to be large or complicated then elaborate on the system of management section because there'll probably be a lot more to say. You may want to include:

◆ How you'll run the business (when and how often you'll do the paperwork and catch up on correspondence, when you'll do your ordering, when and how you'll do your books).

◆ More details on how you'll check product quality control.

◆ What plans you have for customer care and customer feedback.

◆ How you'll manage your time (the proportion spent on admin, design, making, thinking up new lines or services).

Even if your business is tiny and it really is only you and a couple of customers, you should still include a reference to a system of management because it does at least show you have thought about it.

Suppliers

If your business is small and you'll only have a few suppliers, you could include them in Operations or leave them out altogether. But if you're setting up an organic food bar, your supplier list could run to dozens or even hundreds. There'll be local suppliers for food, both raw ingredients and ready-for-sale, plus wholesalers for everything from plates and cutlery to tables, pictures, lighting and pots and pans. Then there'll be the suppliers who'll provide flooring, lavatory fittings, building and plumbing materials. There'll be another set for office supplies, letter heads, business cards, menus, price lists, promotional literature and so on. And there'll be yet another set for basic services such as phone, water, electricity, gas, oil and perhaps wood and coal (for those obligatory open fires in country restaurants).

If this is the case, you need to show in your business plan that you've considered the suppliers and have lists drawn up. This doesn't mean you're stuck with them for life but that you've got enough to get you started.

So here in your business plan include:

◆ likely suppliers
◆ their terms and conditions (cash up front, 30, 60 or 90 day's credit)
◆ probable delivery arrangements (daily, weekly, monthly).

Legalities

Again, this section could easily be swallowed by Operations unless there's plenty to say.

Some businesses will find the legalities more onerous than others. Anything connected with food, health and safety, potentially dangerous machinery and even animals could be particularly affected. Your business plan should show that you're aware of legislation and best practices in your field, and have carried out risk assessments. The legalities to consider will probably include:

◆ your trading status (sole trader, partnership, limited company)
◆ any partnership agreements or company contracts
◆ health and safety requirements
◆ any licences or permissions
◆ any copyright issues.

The numbers

This will probably be the last section of your business plan. If you're writing your plan to try and attract funding, then these figures are going to have to be right, credible and clear. No backer is going to hand over any money until you've shown you're responsible enough to look after it.

You have to show:

+ how much capital, if any, you're putting into the business
+ where your income is coming from
+ what your expenditure is likely to be
+ how much money you need to borrow, if any
+ what security or guarantee you are offering for any loan
+ how you'll repay the money
+ and over what period
+ details of your personal finances.

How much detail to include will depend on your type of business and whether you need to borrow. If you're setting up as a one-woman travelling aromatherapist who can afford to buy the initial stock out of your savings, then you're probably writing your business plan mainly for your own benefit, won't have to borrow and won't have to go into as much detail. If on the other hand you're opening an organic restaurant or well-stocked shop you could be borrowing a sizeable amount, and you'll have to show and justify every relevant number, explaining your assumptions as you go.

Timescale will vary too. Our aromatherapist would probably only do figures for the first year or two, while the organic restaurateur or shop owner would probably have to provide figures for up to the next five years. In either case, logically the first year will be the most detailed: subsequent years can be revised as and when.

The figures you need to prepare are called forecasts and they should be put together on computer spreadsheets. If that's beyond you, then either learn or get someone to do it for you. Spreadsheets display your data clearly, sort categories and do all the sums. Assuming you put in the right numbers in the first place there won't be any mistakes. Anything typewritten or presented on graph paper will look amateurish.

The forecasts to include are:

◆ sales forecast
◆ cashflow forecast
◆ profit and loss forecast.

How to compile them is explained in detail in Chapter 6.

Sales forecast

A sales forecast is exactly as it sounds: a forecast of what you hope to sell in the future. A sales forecast will help you plan for the peaks and troughs in your business, to make sure you have enough stock at busy times and to enable you to use the quieter times to prepare.

It's probably the most difficult section to get right because it's basically down to guesswork. But the more preparation and research you do, the better the guesswork, the more accurate the forecast, then the greater the benefit will be to your business.

Even if you have a figures-phobia and do nothing else, still force yourself to do a sales forecast. It's important you at least begin to get a feel for the financial side, and sales are at the core of your business – the heartbeat if you like.

Some people will question the need for a sales forecast, arguing it's just guesswork and therefore worthless. But if you've done thorough market research, checked what your competitors are up to and costed your own likely expenditure, you should be reasonably accurate. If you do turn out to be wildly wrong, then somewhere down the line you haven't done your homework carefully enough.

Cashflow forecast

A cashflow forecast tries to predict how much money is likely to pass through your business. It's less complicated to put together because it only deals with one element, money. Again, the forecast should help you smooth out the peaks and troughs of your business. You use the information it contains to make sure there's always enough money in your business to continue trading, or in the jargon, you have sufficient working capital.

Any would-be lender or financial backer will look closely at your cashflow forecast to make sure you've taken into account all the key factors, such as the pattern of sales, wages, the cost of raw materials and rent for premises.

Profit and loss forecast

This forecast brings together information taken from the other two forecasts and shows how much profit (or loss) you're likely to make. It sets out how much you think you'll earn from sales against how much you've had to spend and arrives at one figure which should represent your annual income. Hopefully it'll show you in profit.

Personal finances

At some stage in your business plan you will have to include your own personal finances: the level of detail will depend on how relevant they are to your business. If you've thrown every last penny into the business and your family won't eat unless you show a profit within the month, then clearly your personal finances are vital. If on the other hand you have plenty of capital behind you and can afford to go several months or even years without turning a profit, then it's not so important.

At some stage you'll probably need to calculate the minimum amount you need to live on until you make a profit. This is known sometimes as a Personal Survival Budget or PSB. It's simply a total of all your monthly outgoings. You've probably completed similar lists in the past on mortgage or loan application forms. Make sure you include:

- mortgage or rent
- insurance
- council tax
- bills (phone, electricity, gas, oil, water, TV licence)
- outstanding debts (credit cards, car loans)
- housekeeping (food, cleaning, basic maintenance)
- child care
- clothes
- car running costs (tax, insurance, petrol) or other travel costs
- travel, meals out, leisure
- birthdays and Christmas
- emergencies.

The total is often shockingly high. A single person living on their own can easily have monthly outgoings of around £1,000. If you have children it's likely to be much more.

So say your PSB is £1,500 per month. That means your business has to make a minimum profit of £18,000 a year in order for you to just about survive. And that's profit, not turnover or the total amount of money passing through your business.

Remember too that until your business starts making a profit, that £1,500 a month PSB has to come from somewhere else.

SETTING OUT YOUR BUSINESS PLAN

It has to be typewritten. Using a computer is by far the easiest way, though if you're desperate a typewriter will have to do. You may want to email it, so use a format which is readable by most computers, such as Microsoft Word or Acrobat pdf.

There's no set format: what's important is that it's clear and logical, so start with a contents list and then your executive summary. Then sort the chapters into an order which suits you, end with the numbers or forecasts, and at the back include any other support material as an appendix.

If you're unsure about the ideal length, aim for about ten sections and write a page or two of A4 on each. As well as your main headings, don't be afraid to include sub headings and bullet points. Great slabs of text are off-putting and difficult to read. If you think there's no way around this, then at least print it out double-spaced.

The content, detail and length will be decided by the nature of your business and whether it'll be used to try and raise finance. If you're planning a low key, low investment sandwich round for office workers then your plan should be much simpler than someone starting up a furniture making business who needs to borrow to pay for premises, equipment and staff. If you'll be using the plan to try and raise a significant sum of money then it's probably worth paying a professional (business adviser or accountant) to help pull together a really punchy executive summary, management team profile and numbers forecasts.

WHAT TO DO WITH IT

If it's just for your benefit, write it and show it to a couple of people whose opinions you respect and who preferably have had first-hand business experience. Then put it away in a drawer and don't look at it again for two or three weeks while you get on with other things. Then re-read it. Anything strike you as naïve? Wrong? Over-confident? Under-confident? Anything that needs changing as a result of further work you've done in the meantime?

At some stage, regardless of whether the plan is just for you or not, you should also show it to some experts. This will probably include your accountant and perhaps a business adviser if you have one. Ask for their feedback and be prepared to rewrite sections.

Then, if you're going for funding, send it out to back-up loan or grant applications. Many people deciding on these applications will have seen scores of other business plans. They may not give you any money this time, but their comments may help you be more successful next time.

WHAT TO DO IF IT REVEALS SERIOUS FLAWS

Strange but true. If you've written your plan honestly, after having done thorough and realistic research, some of the conclusions may surprise you.

You may have found that:

* There's a viable business but there isn't enough profit.
* Your cashflow isn't sufficient.
* Raw materials are too expensive or too difficult to source.
* One person alone can't run the business.
* Your premises may not be suitable.
* There are already too many people doing what you hope to do.
* You need training or qualifications.
* You need more experience before setting up yourself.

- The business will need more hours than you're prepared to commit.

The list of possibilities is endless.

If any of the above happens, you have three choices:

- Abandon the idea completely and find something else to do.
- Plough on regardless.
- Try to find a way around the problem.

Option one isn't as bleak as it sounds. At this stage you've only lost time and a bit of money. It's far better to be ruthless, cut your losses at this point and find something else that has a better chance of success.

Option two, carrying on regardless, will probably end in disaster. If there is a serious flaw in your business, a decent business plan will expose it. There is absolutely no point in continuing just because 'it feels right', or 'my family and friends all think it's a great idea'. You could get as far as opening for business and sit there waiting for the customers who never arrive.

Option three, finding a way around the problem, is, like most compromises, the best and most painless way forward. So ask for advice from banks, accountants, business advisors and anyone with business experience, and all may not be lost.

UPDATING AND USING YOUR PLAN

A business plan isn't written once and then preserved in aspic for ever. Instead, when you begin trading, use it as an active business tool, as a handbook or manual, which will help you keep your business on track and focused. Refer to it every now and then and use it as a measure to check your progress. For example:

◆ By the start of trading I was hoping to build up a network of six local shops which had agreed to sell my pottery. Are those deals in place?

◆ By Month Three I was hoping to achieve sales of £3,000 a month. Have I reached that target?

◆ By Year Two I was hoping to expand into the next county and agree deals with six more shops. Am I still on track for that?

Some businesses rewrite their plans annually. Certainly if you're planning a big expansion or change of direction you should do it then. Also update your forecasts as predicted sales become reality. The more detail of actual figures achieved, the more accurate your future forecasts will become and the more helpful they'll be to the future of your business.

5

Business Help and
Financial Support

A giant industry has grown up to service the needs of people starting up in business. Various agencies are falling over themselves and each other in order to give you advice and support, and if you're patient, grants and loans.

You could sack all the pen-pushers and return the billions saved straight back to the people. But the Countryside Agency does point out that new businesses stand a better chance of succeeding if they've received professional advice first. Many agencies are also working to dispel the idea that the rural economy is only about farming, food and tourism, leaving everyone else to battle on alone. So perhaps it's money well spent after all.

The many groups, bodies and organisations are funded in different ways, but almost all get their money from the government, Europe, local authorities or the private sector, or any combination of those. Some work behind the scenes formulating policy and you'll probably never have to deal with them. Others provide the upfront services and deal directly with the public.

It's impossible to compile a definitive list of organisations that can help you. Names and aims change almost daily and new ones spring up all the time. There are national, regional and local organisations. But the following should at least provide you with a starting point.

ORGANISATIONS THAT HELP YOU DIRECTLY

Business Link – England

If you want any advice, information or help, one of your first calls should probably be to Business Link. It says it can either answer all your questions about starting up or will find you someone who can. It's partly funded by the Department of Trade and Industry and partly self-financed. There are about 50 Business Link offices in England, basically one per county or pair of counties which are often linked together.

There are several advantages to Business Link:

◆ Its network of offices (known as operators) around the country mean its staff have local knowledge and can offer relevant local advice.

◆ Its services are usually free.

- Because Business Link operators have no affiliations, they offer impartial advice and have no commercial axe to grind.

- Business Link offices have up-to-date lists of grants available in your local area.

Business Link grants

The lists provided aren't definitive because they only include government-funded grants but they do give a good idea of what's around. As examples, here are three plucked at random from the Devon Business Link list of November 2004:

- Community Services Grant. Available to anyone who provides the sole shop, pub or garage in a rural settlement unless there are two enterprises clearly doing different things, e.g. butcher and baker, in which case they can both apply. Grants of up to 50 per cent, or £500 to £25,000, are available. The grant money has to be spent on things like improving access to the premises, modernising the sales area or buying essential equipment.

- RABBIT – Remote Area Broadband Inclusion Trial. This promotes the use of broadband internet in areas not covered by ADSL or cable. The small business or trader can apply for £700 or the fees for the first 12 months, whichever is the lower.

- Sub Post Office Start Up Scheme. A fund that can provide up to £20,000 if alternative funding isn't available. The proposed sub post office must be in a community of less than 10,000 people, where a sub post office has closed in the last 18 months or is likely to do so in the next six months.

The Business Link offices around the country are autonomous and don't always provide the same services. It's worth asking if they offer a personalised grant search facility. Devon does, and charges a reasonable £50 plus VAT for it.

To contact your local Business Link office, log onto the website www.businesslink.gov.uk and enter your post code (top left of the page) to show the area you're in.

Scotland

Lowland Scotland
In Lowland Scotland the Business Link equivalent is called Business Gateway. It provides help and advice for people starting up in business and for those who're already up and running. Its website is clear, comprehensive and easy to follow. There are sections on financing your business, tax, VAT and national insurance, building the right team, growth and so on. It also offers seminars, workshops and business health checks.

Website: www.bgateway.com
Tel: 0845 609 6611

Highlands and Islands
Here you talk to Highlands and Islands Enterprise. There are already about 19,000 existing businesses in the Highlands and Islands so there's obviously business potential. HIE offers business support and advice, training programmes, help for community projects and so on. The services are usually filtered through the ten Local Enterprise Companies (LECs), which once again is good because local is almost always best. This is another clear, well-run and apparently up-to-date site.

Website: www.hie.co.uk
Tel: 01463 234171

Wales
In Wales the organisation to talk to is Business Eye.

Website: www.businesseye.org.uk
Tel: 08457 969798

Northern Ireland
In Northern Ireland it's called Invest Northern Ireland.

Website: www.investni.com
Tel: 028 9023 9090

Enterprise agencies
Enterprise agencies cover much of the same work as Business Link but they say their local agencies act (even) more independently and can offer more specific advice relevant to your local area. The help and expertise offered in Cornwall, for example, would be very different to that provided in Watford or east London.

There is a network of enterprise agencies across England. The co-ordinating organisation is the National Federation of Enterprise Agencies. The brief is to encourage economic regeneration. In 2003 (the last available figures), enterprise agencies say they helped more than 20,000 new businesses start up.

Enterprise agencies specifically target small businesses that are preparing to start trading, offering them advice, information, counselling and training on the best way to begin, and how to sustain and grow the business once it's underway. Usefully there's also a mentoring service which pairs up experienced business people with novices. Some local enterprise agencies also have loan funds and access to other financial backing. Check directly with your own local agency.

Website: www.nfea.com

J4B

This is an excellent website which allows you to do your own search for grants. It's remarkably clearly laid-out and easy to follow. Its database contains details of government and European grants available for small and medium sized businesses. The site is one of the main alternatives if you don't want to use an agency.

Website: www.j4b.co.uk

Chambers of Commerce

These have largely reinvented themselves over the last few years, shedding their stuffy and conservative (small c) image. They've taken on both a campaigning and a training role. According to the chambers' collective website, they are 'the premier commercial provider of skills and workforce development training to business, delivering to tens of thousands of employees each year'. And it goes on: 'They are also one of the largest government funded training providers in Great Britain, training more than 13,000 youth and adult trainees during the last contract year'. The chambers emphasise their training is designed to reflect local needs, for example the production of leather goods in the Midlands, glass manufacturing in Lancashire or working on the land or with animals in rural areas.

So take them at their word. Contact your local chamber of commerce and see what it can do for you. As an added incentive, the chambers say that if you become a member you get access to good deals on things like car and health insurance and save more cash than the price of your membership fee.

You may think they're not really for you, especially if you're in arts or crafts, but don't automatically dismiss them. Whatever you're doing it's still about running a business and your local chamber of commerce will have many members who have a lifetime's experience in that. It's also a good opportunity for a bit of networking.

Website: www.chamberonline.co.uk

Federation of Small Businesses

The Federation of Small Businesses (FSB) offers a wide range of services and support to its 185,000 members. Even if you're not a natural joiner it's still worth looking at its website.

The FSB is non-profit-making and non-party political. It doesn't offer detailed advice, training and information in the same way as Business Link or the enterprise agencies do: instead it provides a more general range of services. One of the big benefits is the FSB's legal helpline which operates 24 hours a day. According to its website the helpline took more than 100,000 calls in 2003 (the last available figures), the majority on employment issues. If you're going into anything contentious the helpline alone could justify your membership fee.

Via membership you also get access to good deals on things like financial planning and medical and travel insurance. And there could be other one-off benefits. During 2001, the FSB distributed half a million pounds in interest-free loans to members who were in financial difficulties because of the Foot and Mouth outbreak.

The FSB is also a vigorous campaigner and lobbyist on behalf of small businesses everywhere so it's generally a good organisation to support.

Website: www.fsb.org.uk

Rural Community Councils

Rural Community Councils (RCCs) offer a wide range of services, including the administering of various grants, to anyone living in the countryside. There's basically one per county. Check the internet or the phone book for your local council. Check particularly for their resource centres which are often good places to hear first about the best local grants and loans around and the best people to approach for support and advice.

Local and regional bodies

There are many purely local or regional groups. Your local Business Link or enterprise agency should point you in the right direction, otherwise look in the phone book, phone your local authority or do an internet search.

The *Herefordshire Partnership* is a good example of what's around at the local level. Funded by the local unitary authority, regional development agency and European money, it covers just what it says in the name and isn't stretched to cover its obvious twin of Worcestershire. The Herefordshire Partnership, whose unofficial mantra is 'local and lovely', says its success is down to knowing who's who locally and understanding how things work.

It's a signposting organisation so it listens to what people have to say and then puts them in touch with groups who can help, either with advice or grants. As well as all the usual links, the Partnership also has contacts with similar groups in neighbouring Gloucestershire, Worcestershire, Shropshire and Wales, as well as with organisations like the Forestry Commission. It helps around 500 start-up and young businesses every year, publishes a funding directory and runs a website. The service is free.

Tel: 01432 261792

Email: projectdevelopment@herefordshire.gov.uk

The Prince's Trust

Unfortunately you have to be under 30 to benefit from the Prince's Trust. But if you are it is worth getting in touch. The emphasis is on helping people who've been disadvantaged in some way, but it also takes on the long-term unemployed. The Trust offers training, personal development, business start-up support, mentoring and advice.

Grants and loans

- The Prince's Trust offers up to £500 to help the applicant get more education and training.

- There are cash grants for groups working on community projects.

- Low interest loans, grants and other business start-up support are available. Mostly it goes to the unemployed who've been refused funding elsewhere. It's slightly different in Scotland: check the Prince's Trust website.

Website: www.princes-trust.org.uk/

Case study: The Yorkshire outdoor instructor

Ian Cullen is a freelance outdoor instructor from Otley, West Yorkshire. He leads groups on the Yorkshire Dales in team building and mental challenge exercises based on activities such as orienteering, walking, climbing and caving.

How did you start?

A friend and I talked about opening a café as a centre for cyclists, walkers and climbers. We realised the café was a rubbish idea and concentrated on the outdoor stuff. In 1990 we got a grant from the Prince's Trust and started a company to take business managers out on the Dales. We were lucky because in our first year we got involved in training teams for a big national challenge trophy. We trained a team from Powergen and they won! But in the early 1990s the recession hit.

What then?

My business partner went out and got a job. I plugged on for a bit and eventually went freelance rather than run my own business which saves a lot of time in marketing. I started running elements in other people's events. It was successful and I did a lot of travelling. I worked in the USA, France and Dubai, but then the children came along and you can't keep travelling.

What do you do now?

Some outdoor teambuilding for companies, though mainly I work with residents of bail hostels, taking them out on the Dales and helping raise their self-esteem by exposing them to challenges. There are often literacy problems so the symbols and use of numbers in map reading also helps with that.

Why did you end up with this type of job?

It's a lifestyle choice. I'm not motivated to make lots of money. Overheads are low. I've never had a big mortgage or any debt apart from that. And I never did much marketing. It was word of mouth and over the years I developed a good reputation.

Email: iecullen@aol.com

WiRE – Women in Rural Enterprise

WiRE is a business membership club for women. This is an excellent service with a clear and informative website: it's just a shame if you're a man. It was founded by Izzy Warren Smith, a lecturer at the rural-leaning Harper Adams University in Shropshire, after she conducted research and realised that many existing support organisations were too man-orientated and didn't allow time for carers' duties that many women have. She identified several particular problems facing women who were having to diversify because of falling farm incomes:

* lack of access to finance
* lack of confidence
* not being taken seriously
* rural isolation
* lack of rural business support.

WiRE helps members find grants, provides a mentoring service and has negotiated favourable rates with one of the high street banks. It organises events and talks: 'Making the most of your website' is typical and sounds particularly useful. And its own website has a good county-based directory which anyone can look at. It also provides good and sensible general business tips on employee legislation, planning, health and safety, insurance, equality and so on.

Website: www.wireuk.org

ARTS AND CRAFTS

Crafts Council

This is a useful organisation for anyone going into crafts and/or thinking about opening up their own workshop. Like Business Link and others, if it can't help you it'll probably be able to find you someone who can. The Crafts Council is an independent body funded by the Arts Council England (there are sister organisations in Scotland and Wales), and its job, in its words, is to promote contemporary crafts and to provide services to craftspeople and the public.

It has a useful database and resource centre which offers advice on legalities, funding, availability of studios and so on. An example could be a stone mason calling up to check his position on public liability insurance. Some of the straightforward research is free, otherwise there's a small charge.

The council doesn't usually offer specific business and/or start-up advice unless you receive one of its grants or awards, though it does occasionally organise training events.

Grants, loans and business support

The Council's funding packages appear to be comprehensive and wide-ranging for those lucky enough to receive them. Many grants and loans have a short life, but the Crafts Council's Development Award (previously the Setting Up Scheme) has been around for more than 30 years so should be good for another few yet.

The Development Award offers:

- a general grant (£2,500 in November 2004)

- an equipment grant of up to £5,000 (you have to pay half) – a third of this can be used to buy marketing equipment such as cameras or computers

- one-to-one support from a Professional Development Officer

- access to a creative mentor

- a residential course in business training, aimed specifically at the small creative traders and concentrating on marketing, PR, intellectual property and financial management

- one thousand free postcards

- two studio visits by their designated Professional Development Officer who'll assess equipment, workshop suitability, and offer advice on work, direction and sales opportunities

- inclusion on the Crafts Council's Photostoreâ (sic), a visual database available to groups like architects and the media.

The Crafts Council claims excellent results for this scheme. According to its research among recipients, 100 per cent are still in business after four years and 50 per cent after six years – much better, it says, than for start-up businesses generally.

The Council also runs a scheme called Next Move. At the time of writing (November 2004) its funding isn't as secure, but the Council says it hopes to continue something along these lines. Next Move is aimed at designer-makers, i.e. people who design and who are also involved in the making or manufacturing process. Broadly, the scheme aims to give arts and design graduates a head start in launching their businesses. It provides work space, equipment, grants, training and promotion opportunities in a host college. In detail:

- rent-free studio space in a college department
- a maintenance grant of £6,000 (November 2004)
- a business equipment grant of £1,000
- in-depth support and business training
- access to specialist equipment.

There are also other types of grants and loans available. The Council will also help you track down other funding which may be regional or local to you.

Website: www.craftscouncil.org.uk

AGRICULTURE/FARMING

There's a whole separate support and funding network out there for anyone who works in farming or agriculture-related businesses. Not surprisingly, many are linked to Defra, the Department for Environment, Food and Rural Affairs.

This book is not about farming: there are plenty of those around already. However, if you are considering an intensive polytunnel operation, smallholding or livestock rearing business, then there are a couple of places where you could start.

Once again, some organisations are concerned only with policy and with overseeing and co-ordinating the work of other groups, so it's important you identify where you can get direct help and support.

Rural Enterprise Scheme

This comes under the wing of Defra and is a wide-ranging scheme. It does lean towards helping farmers diversify and adapt to changing markets, but there are many other projects or businesses it will get involved in as well. Certainly if you're a rural trader, local craftsperson, or even working on a local community project, then it's worth speaking to them.

Here are some examples of what the Scheme will support:

◆ Encouragement for tourist and craft activities. Projects could include the marketing and promotion of local tourist initiatives or helping to provide on-farm visitor attractions.

◆ Diversification. Here this covers helping farmers or landowners move into new or non-mainstream crops or the conversion of farm buildings to new and non-agricultural uses.

◆ Conservation of rural heritage. This is about promoting the revival or expansion of local artisan crafts (thatching, hedge-laying, stone masonry, wood carving) and the renovation of historic village buildings or the promotion of village museums.

Any eligible project has to be sustainable and not have any negative impact on the environment. The scheme is available across England except in the Objective One areas, which are Merseyside, South Yorkshire, Cornwall and the Isles of Scilly, which have their own arrangements (see below).

Famously, many grant applications can take months to be approved. However, according to its website, there is a Rural Enterprise Scheme (RES) fast track system. Smaller projects that have applied for grants of up to £15,000 will get a decision within a month. All the usual criteria still have to be met though: the forms still have to be completed, a formal business plan submitted, and the applicant or project still has to meet the eligibility criteria.

Farm Business Advisory Service (FBAS)
This is a useful support service for farmers and some other growers which unfortunately may not exist for much longer. At the time of writing its future was not secure after the spring of 2005. Though it may not continue in its current form, a similar service could replace it so it's worth checking if you think you may benefit.

FBAS (pronounced eff-bass) is funded by Defra and managed through Business Link. While it is aimed mainly at farmers, other growers may still find themselves eligible. You have to spend at least 75 per cent of your time working on the land, be a farmer or grower in England and have an agricultural holding number. Even if you meet these conditions you may still not benefit. FBAS doesn't have a bottomless pit of money or time and does have to prioritise. Basically if you farm 300 acres or have 15 acres of intensive polytunnels you're more likely to get help than someone with five acres and a flock of hobby sheep.

FBAS offers what it calls an on-farm diagnostic service to provide a 'health check'. In English, it means it'll send someone along with a fresh eye to have a look at what you're doing and to help you put together a business strategy for the future. This could include:

- suggestions on improving business methods
- possible diversification
- or, ominously, 'Exit Routes'.

A typical visit will last about four days and is free. It's particularly useful because you get the benefit of some detailed, expert and independent free advice which in industry would cost tens of thousands of pounds in consultants' time.

Website via: www.businesslink.gov.uk
Tel: 0845 600 9006

HOW TO IMPROVE YOUR CHANCES OF GETTING A GRANT

While potentially there is a lot of money out there you can't expect to rely on handouts, either to get started or to bail you out of trouble. You have to be seen to be doing a lot of hard work yourself first: basically, the more effort you put in, the more likely you are to get something. Remember that, as in life, you never get anything for nothing.

You can dramatically increase your chances of getting some money by applying as soon as possible. Most pots of money are not bottomless and it's usually first come first served. So find out how and when the money is allocated: is it decided at the beginning of every calendar year, every financial year, every quarter or only at the beginning of a scheme? Either way, get your application in fast.

There are two principle types of funding you can apply for:

◆ **Grants**. You are given a sum of money, effectively a gift, which you don't have to pay back. Don't get too excited though: grants will often be for relatively small amounts, the application process can be exhausting and there may be tough conditions attached.

◆ **Loans**. You borrow money, either interest-free or at a preferential rate (known as a 'soft loan'), and pay it back at some stage in the future when your business is earning more money.

Every grant or loan application is different, but on the whole expect to do at least one of the following:

◆ Fill out a lengthy application form, but don't be put off if the end justifies the means.

◆ Submit an up-to-date business plan, including a sales forecast.

◆ Hand over your latest accounts.

◆ Prepare a formal proposal and/or presentation.

◆ Attend an interview.

◆ Be prepared to match whatever funding you're hoping for. For example, if you're applying for a £500 grant to buy a computer, you may have to show you have your own £500 to put in.

Other points to take into account:

◆ Many grants will only be given for specific items. You're more likely to be able to use a loan to put into the general pot of money you need to keep your business afloat.

◆ Don't expect ever to receive 100 per cent of the cost of doing something. If you are successful in your application, you're likely to receive between 15 and 50 per cent.

◆ Be prepared to wait. The decision-making process could take some time. Business Link warns that some government grants can take several months to be approved. If you're desperate, then you need to look for alternative sources of money in the short term.

◆ Business-related grants and loans are a hugely complicated area and can change almost daily. If you do see something that suits you, don't hang around, get your application in fast. Equally, if you can't find anything, then it's probably worth looking around again a month or two later.

Applications can take days to prepare: a scribbled sheet of A4 won't get you anywhere. So weigh up the benefits of the grant or loan against the time it'll take you to prepare your submission. If you spend 12 hours or one and a half working days preparing an application for a £50 grant towards the cost of a photocopier, are you actually better off using that time to work on your business? Of course you are.

With probably the only honourable exception of the J4B site, you're generally better off looking for organisations that will help you with grant application forms. They'll help you identify the grants suitable for you in the first place and then check to make sure you meet the eligibility criteria, which can often be robust. In other words, most organisations are very fussy about who they give their money to.

ORGANISATIONS THAT HELP YOU INDIRECTLY

Of the various government departments, the Department of Trade and Industry (DTI) and Defra have the most responsibility for small businesses, so it's worth looking at their websites for general background:

Websites: www.dti.gov.uk and www.defra.gov.uk

The Countryside Agency

This is a good and worthwhile organisation but of absolutely no direct help to the small trader just starting up. The Countryside Agency is a public body funded by Defra. Its main roles are to make suggestions and advise the government on its policy for rural areas, and to act as a co-ordinator and facilitator for the countless smaller groups which work in this field. In short, it produces advisory papers, reports, surveys and research papers by the score for the benefit of other bureaucrats. It's not there to help you write your business plan, advise you on the best delivery van to buy or show you the most effective way to lay out a market stall. But the Countryside Agency is at least batting for you. One of its other principal roles is to make sure the countryside receives at least as much help and support as urban areas.

So if you're interested in policy or the wider picture then its website is worth reading, if only because it shows which way the government of the day is likely to be thinking. While you're getting started and struggling to find premises, your first suppliers and worrying about cash flow, government policy will probably seem irrelevant. But national policies do affect the chances of your business succeeding, and if there are any nasty surprises coming up, then it is better to at least be warned.

Website: www.countryside.gov.uk

Small Business Service

The Small Business Service (SBS) (part of the DTI) is at the time of writing the parent or overseer of Business Link in England. It is another body that looks after policy and regulation and again is not really the place to go if you have specific questions about your fledgling home ironing service. But its website is however written – by the government's standards – in fairly plain English and is quite useful if you are interested in the wider picture.

Website: www.sbs.gov.uk

OBJECTIVE ONE AND TWO AREAS

Objective One and Two funding is money from Europe that is designed to help the economic regeneration of poorer areas. As a general rule, individual small traders won't benefit directly: the money is usually funnelled through larger businesses and organisations and is then spent to benefit the community.

Conceivably, if you're going into tourism or planning to bring lots of jobs to one of the designated areas, then you may possibly get something. But it's far more likely you'd benefit indirectly. For example, grant money is often spent on improving local environments or establishing new facilities. These in turn bring more people to an area, make it more attractive and therefore in theory increase your number of potential customers.

Generally, Objective One and Two status is positive news for a region because it does mean that millions of pounds is pouring in. But also remember that a region had to be poor and economically deprived in the first place in order to benefit.

Objective One areas are the poorest and therefore receive the most money. They are: Cornwall and the Isles of Scilly, South Yorkshire, Merseyside, West Wales and the Valleys. There are nine Objective Two areas in England, one in each region which contains a government office. Both programmes run for seven years, 2000–06.

OTHER SOURCES OF HELP AND ADVICE

The National Rural Knowledge Exchange is, at the time of writing, a recent consortium of 14 universities and colleges whose aim is to promote the development of the rural economy by providing web-based and physical access to sources of technology, innovative ideas and business advice. Its linked website, www.nationalrural.org, is due to be fully up and running by mid-summer 2005.

Other sources of advice include the obvious ones which can easily be overlooked. Check out your bank manager and your bank's small business adviser, solicitor, accountant, the Inland Revenue, Customs and Excise and the Health and Safety Executive.

There are two schools of thought about advice from these types of sources. The first is that they've probably had years of dealing with other small businesses and will have built up a huge reservoir of experience and wisdom on which to draw. The counter view, reported by some small business people, is that bank managers and the like have no direct first-hand experience of business ('cushioned by a salary and safe pension' is how one put it), and don't have any idea of the harsh economic realities in the real world.

6

The Money
Part 1: Before You Start Trading

BUSINESS BANK ACCOUNTS

If your business will be tiny or you're likely to handle only a couple
of large-ish cheques a month, then you can probably get away with
putting them through your usual account. Otherwise you're going to
have to open a business account, and unfortunately they're not free.
You'll usually get a period of free introductory banking with a
business start-up account, but after that you basically pay in some
way per transaction. Shop around and don't necessarily stick with
the bank you have your domestic account with. The banks will want
your business so should negotiate, within reason, on the terms.
Certainly don't accept the first package they offer until you've at

least tried to argue for a better deal. It won't do any harm to try – after all, you're in business now.

If you're likely to have a lot of transactions passing through the account, then make sure you get weekly, or at least fortnightly, statements. You'll need to keep track of what's been received, what's still owing and what's bounced, and a month is too long to wait to find out.

When you come to open an account, the bank will probably ask to see your business plan plus details of where your start-up money is coming from. You'll also have to provide all the usual ID. If you want more than one signature on the account, you'll have to provide a list of names and examples of their signatures. You also need to say in what combination the signatures have to be used, for example two signatures per transaction.

Forget all the horror stories you've ever heard about bank managers and try to be their friend. It's far better if you maintain a good relationship with them. So:

- Meet the person managing your account.
- Keep in touch with them.
- Send them a copy of your annual accounts.
- If you ever rewrite your business plan send them that too.

Go and see your bank manager immediately if you think your business could be in trouble. Take them into your confidence and tell them about your plans to sort things out. They'll be immediately more sympathetic than if you wait for the cheques to start bouncing. You'll also stand a far better chance of borrowing your way out of trouble if you're seen to be managing your account sensibly.

THE START-UP MONEY YOU'LL NEED

Sit down and write out a list of the equipment you already have: you'll probably have more than you realise, items like a PC, printer, scanner, phone line, mobile phone and car. Then write out a second list of what you're going to have to buy and price that up. Include the cost of:

◆ stock and/or raw materials
◆ taking on any premises
◆ equipment
◆ office administration, marketing and advertising.

◆ Add to that how much you and your family need to live on until the business makes a profit. Depending on your business, this could be for a month, a quarter, six months, a year, or even longer.
◆ Add to that an amount for contingencies and disasters. Again this will depend on your type of business, but it should probably be equivalent to at least 15–20 per cent of the above total.

Then think about how much money you have and how much you need to borrow.

The timetable

Not all new equipment has to be bought immediately. It will help if you can stagger the purchases over several months. Think about drawing up a timetable, which should at least make you think about the options. Something like:

◆ January of next year: buy second vehicle.
◆ Summer of next year: replace laptop and buy two new printers.
◆ Beginning of the year after: replace industrial ovens/kiln/sewing machine/lawn mower.

HOW BUSINESS BORROWING WORKS

Most businesses, rural or otherwise, need some money to get started. The good news is that it's probably never been easier to borrow money, and on reasonable terms. The bad news is that the form filling that goes with it has probably never been more complicated. This is especially true if you decide to apply for any grants or loans (see Chapter 5).

A potentially fatal but all too common mistake of small businesses starting up is to be under-funded. This often means that you run out of money too early, before your business is on its feet and starting to show a profit.

Another issue to address right at the beginning is that there's nothing wrong with business borrowing. In our personal lives the usual best advice is to save up for something you want to buy. This advice is almost universally ignored, hence the astronomical level of personal debt built up on credit cards in the last few years. But in business it's accepted practice to borrow, especially if it helps your business grow faster than it could otherwise have done. Or look at it another way: is the development of your business being held back because you don't have enough money to expand?

What it boils down to is being able to borrow money and make it earn more money than it's costing you in interest to borrow. A crude example of this is in the domestic housing market where in recent years it's been possible to take out a mortgage that charges, say, five per cent interest, but which you use to buy a property that appreciates at ten per cent a year.

So use the same example in business.

You're going into wine importing. You're able to buy 300 cases at £50 a case. You should sell the cases on at £80 each. Your expenses are £20 a case, so you expect to make £10 profit on each one. That's a £3,000 profit on an initial investment of £15,000, or a return of 20 per cent. As long as you can borrow money to buy more wine at an interest rate of less than 20 per cent then you're making a profit. The difference, or margin, between the interest rate and the return you get is your profit. So, the more money you borrow, the more money you make.

This is simplified because there are different ways of calculating interest on borrowings and different ways of calculating profit on investments (if you take the £20 per case costs into account your profit is less), but it illustrates the general principle.

WHO TO BORROW FROM

A lot will depend on the type of business you're going into and what you need the money for. You also need to think about whether you'd be prepared to hand over some of the business to a third party in order to raise finance.

Loans

The most obvious place to start is your bank or building society. This is a good, safe and easy method of borrowing: the terms should be reasonable, and as long as you can keep up the repayments there should be no nasty surprises lurking around the corner.

Loans are probably most suitable for buying tangible items (caterer's industrial oven, potter's wheel) and office equipment because you'll know in advance how much money you need to borrow and it's unlikely to change. Loans are not as appropriate for general running expenses because you may not need one all the time but would still have to pay interest on it.

The main advantages of loans are that they're for fixed periods, you'll know what your repayments are and can budget accordingly. The downside is that you'll need to have a regular flow of cash through your business to meet the repayments, and that the loan will probably have to be secured (guaranteed) against something, usually the business or perhaps occasionally your home. This means that if for any reason you fail to continue paying the loan, whatever has been put up as security can be forfeited. In extreme cases the lender could close down your business or force the sale of your home.

Overdrafts

Overdrafts are more flexible than loans, but you pay for the privilege with higher interest rates. Overdrafts are more suitable for day-to-day running costs because you only borrow and pay interest on what you need. It doesn't make sense to use overdrafts to buy fixed price items because it's more expensive.

You probably need to be more disciplined to operate an overdraft successfully. Just because your bank has agreed an overdraft limit of X it doesn't mean you should immediately go out and spend up to that limit. Instead, think of it as a safety net, only to be used if necessary. Also be aware that lenders will charge a higher interest rate if they think that you could be a risky prospect, i.e. you may default.

Overdrafts are usually secured or backed by business assets. Once again, if you default your lender could call in those assets and your business could be threatened.

Loans from family or friends

If your business is low key, you don't need much to tide you over and you don't want to go to the trouble of formally applying for loans or overdrafts, then borrowing from family or friends could be the answer. Mixing your business and personal life can be catastrophic, but there are ways to manage it which should minimise the risk of disaster.

Always, always, put the deal in writing. In the document make it crystal clear you are borrowing X amount over Y term and will pay Z interest. If you're borrowing a large sum of money it's probably worth talking to your solicitor.

There are several advantages to borrowing from family members or friends. On the whole, they're likely to be more supportive, the process should be much quicker and simpler, and any benefit from the loan will stay in the family or at least out of the clutches of the high street lenders. But on the downside, the family member or friend may want to become involved in your business, relations can become strained if you fail to meet any of the payments, and if your business fails then the investor could lose all their money.

You have to decide whether the ease and flexibility of borrowing from family or friends outweighs the risk of something going badly wrong.

Shares

If your business is larger and you'll need more capital, you could consider issuing shares. Businesses with high start-up costs, restaurants, anything property or land-based, or anything that needs to carry a lot of stock from the beginning, would fall into this category. Essentially a share issue buys someone a stake in your company. They get a say in the running and a share of profits (usually proportional to their investment) while you get their money.

By far and away the biggest problem is that the more shares you sell the less control over your own company that you have. Corporate history is littered with examples of desperate battles between shareholders and management. This probably sounds a bit extreme if you're only considering selling a couple of shares, representing no more than four or five per cent, in your organic café to your faithful mum or best friend. But it is an example of what can happen if you don't think things through.

Selling shares is best for raising money for larger and long-term projects. It could help you propel your business into another league or it could help you get started in the first place. Perhaps you've been selling your home-produced chutneys and relishes at farmers' markets and craft fairs but would now like to buy premises and open your own small shop. Or maybe your dream has always been to run your own market garden. You have the expertise and the seeds but can't afford the acres.

Shares are good because you're not taking on debt and there are no regular repayments to make, but you have to decide if you're happy to part with a stake in your business in return.

Joining forces

It may be a bit premature to consider joint ventures while your business is still in its infancy, or even before it's been born, but it's an idea always to keep at the back of your mind. Joint ventures are basically two or more businesses that get together, pooling resources and expertise, in order to reach a particular goal. The risks and the rewards are shared. Joint ventures are usually different from formal partnerships:

◆ Joint ventures can bring together complementary businesses while partnerships usually involve all partners doing essentially the same thing (solicitors, for example).

◆ Joint ventures are usually set up for fixed periods while partnerships tend to be open-ended.

◆ Partnerships are usually profit-driven whereas joint ventures may have a different goal, such as expansion and benefiting from the other business's markets.

There are many businesses out there that naturally complement each other: tree surgery and landscaping, bakery and cheese-making, ceramicists and artists, illustrators and writers, and so on. There are several advantages to going into business together:

◆ You can cross-refer customers.
◆ You can gain access to new markets.
◆ You can pool resources (share shop or workspace).
◆ You can share knowledge, experience and expertise.
◆ You can share the risk.
◆ You can give each other moral support.
◆ You should be able to expand more quickly.
◆ You may be able to share staff (admin or clerical staff, counter help).

But there are several very obvious disadvantages too:

◆ You and your partner may have different ideas about where the business should be going.

◆ There may be a clash over different management styles.

◆ You may lose absolute control over your side of the business.

◆ Your money may be at risk (depending on how the joint venture has been set up).

Whichever way you do it, there must be a written agreement between the parties before you start working together, making it clear what the aims and objectives are. It's just as important, and maybe even more so, if you're going into business with a friend and would like to stay friends. It's probably safest that a solicitor draws up the agreement.

Equity finance

More business jargon, and probably only for those who need really big sums of money to get started anyway.

There are two methods here:

◆ **Business angels**. Angels come in all forms (they back West End theatre) but in this case they tend to be private investors who invest in small to medium sized businesses that have excellent potential to grow. Typically angels invest from around £10,000 to £100,000 in new businesses or those in the very early stages of expansion. In return they'll want to receive a significant proportion of your profits.

◆ **Venture capitalists (VCs)**. These are companies that are prepared to lend large amounts of money to fledgling businesses. However, you need an excellent management track record, a strong team around you and a first class business plan. Unless you're planning to found a global enterprise (after having done it successfully at least once before) then don't hold out too many hopes on this one.

But if you do think either of the above is a realistic and serious option which is at least worth exploring, then talk to a business adviser or your bank manager.

In business, there's no real way of escaping the jargon. Like any profession it revels in its jargon, which is designed to make insiders feel like important members of the club while outsiders are kept out in the cold. But you're going to have to get used to it. Even if you're capitalist-averse, hate everything that business stands for, and are going into trade on co-operative or sharing principles, you are still going to have to pick up and learn at least some of the terms.

THE ART OF PRICING

Pricing is about far more than what something cost to make or supply, with a bit on top for profit (unless you're planning an unlikely career in gasket manufacturing). Pricing says a lot about a product or service. It talks about status, luxury-quotient, the type of person likely to buy it and where it's positioned in its sector.

If you price something too cheaply then customers will be suspicious, wondering if it's not quite up to scratch, shoddy and poorly made. Different rules apply to basic foodstuffs and household items where cheapness and value for money can sometimes be a virtue. But on the whole the psychology of higher prices applies to most things.

If you're not convinced, have a look around your own home, your furniture, kitchen ware and other possessions, your clothes, your children's clothes, shoes, perhaps jewellery, and certainly the cars. How many times did you reject something cheaper in favour of what you ended up buying? There are endless excuses we make to ourselves: it'll last longer, it's a good investment, it's more hard wearing, it won't date, it's better designed so more useful ... ultimately, however, we've been seduced into thinking that by the price tag.

The Aga is a classic example of pricing and branding snobbery. It's a brilliantly engineered, quality object which does exactly what it's designed to, i.e. be a cooker and a source of heat, but is it worth paying a premium price? There are far cheaper ways of cooking and heating but people are still queueing up to buy them. Ask yourself why.

That's not to say you think of a figure for your own product or skill, stick a zero on the end and sit back and wait for the bucks to roll in. But pricing is an extremely important element and one that you should be thinking about right at the beginning. So, factors to consider:

◆ How much did it cost to make or produce (raw materials and labour)?

◆ Or, if providing a service, what is the minimum per hour or day you would work for in order not to starve?

- What about other costs – power, heating and lighting, admin and vehicle charges?

- What do you consider a *reasonable* profit margin, 10, 15, 25 or 50 per cent?

- Are there many other competitors nearby?

- What do they charge?

- How *necessary* is your product or skill? (Are you the only skilled and available sheep shearer within 20 miles?)

- How desperate are customers likely to be for your product or skill? Do you make the only decent bread in your valley while the nearest supermarket is 15 miles away?

- Is your product or skill a luxury, the first thing to go if there's to be belt-tightening? Handmade velvet-trimmed shoes, fresh cream truffles, bespoke rustic furniture, £500 footstools? Pedicurist or aromatherapist?

- Is there any rarity value in what you're offering? Are you a skilled portraitist who'll work in oils and spend many hours on a single commission?

- How well-off is your typical customer likely to be?

- Will they have much disposable income?

- Are they likely to show loyalty to your product or skill?

- Are you working and living in an economically healthy area?

- Is your product or skill weather-dependent?

- Is the cost of any of your raw materials likely to be volatile?

When you've decided on your price then ask yourself: 'Would I buy this?' because at the end of the day that's the only question that matters.

There's always scope for amending your prices as you go, but it doesn't look great if there are great swings in prices or too many changes too close together. Small increases, which can be blamed on inflation, probably look better than small decreases, which will only make you look desperate. If in doubt, pitch prices on the low side, at least at the beginning.

But you must never be afraid to increase prices when your costs increase, i.e. pass on the rises to your customer. And you must review your prices at least once a year.

FIXED AND VARIABLE COSTS

Costs are critical when it comes to setting your prices. Obviously you need to know how much something has cost you to produce before you know how much to charge. There's no point in taking a wild guess, or even an educated one, because it'll probably be far more than you think. Costs are divided into categories:

Fixed costs

These costs remain the same and are not affected by your level of work (how many items you are producing or number of customers you have). They include:

- business rates
- insurances
- vehicle running costs
- rent or lease charges
- cost of employing staff.

Semi-variable costs

These are costs that vary and are probably not known in advance. They are affected by your level of business activity. They include:

- office or admin costs, such as power, heating and lighting
- phone bills
- postage
- advertising, promotions, marketing
- vehicle maintenance and servicing
- fuel costs.

Variable costs

These costs vary directly with the output of your business – for example, food costs for a restaurateur or the cost of wood for a furniture maker.

You also need to include your own earnings in there somewhere. Which sort of cost it is will be decided by how dependent you are on your business to keep afloat. If you have to take out something each month then it's a fixed cost: if you can afford to only take out cash when there's some spare then it's a variable cost.

BREAK-EVEN POINT

Once you've established your costs you can work out your break-even. The formal definition of the break-even point is when the volume of sales creates sufficient revenue to equal total costs. In English it just means the point at which you go into profit. So this will be a combination of costs or overheads, plus the cost of your raw materials, plus an amount for your time, equalling what you've made in sales.

MARK-UP

Once you've got your break-even you can decide on your mark-up.

This is usually expressed as a percentage of the break-even. For example, if you can make a stained glass window at a break-even price of £100 but decide you want to sell it for £150, your mark-up is 50 per cent.

There's no magic formula for deciding on your mark-up: many factors will decide it. But it basically boils down to a couple of words that underpin the whole structure of our economy: supply and demand. If a customer wants your product, they will pay for it. If there's a plentiful supply then you'll have to charge less in order to attract the customer. But if there's less supply and the demand is still there you can charge more. Or look at it another way: volume sales equals lower mark-up.

Millions of words have been written on supply and demand, whole forests felled to supply the paper, thousands of jobs supported by its endless analysis and application, even wars fought over the principle of a demand-led economy. You can spend a lifetime considering it (and plenty do).

But ultimately your mark-up mostly still depends on a lot of guesswork and what you think you can get away with. Look at what your closest competitors are doing, don't be too outrageous or too greedy, or too timid for that matter, and settle on a percentage that seems about right. And congratulate yourself on not wasting months reading economics text books.

MARKET TESTING

This means going out and selling a little of whatever it is your business does before committing yourself wholeheartedly to the venture. If you want to be a dry stone waller then start off by advertising in the local paper and see what response you get. Or if you hope to be producing marmalades and chutneys on a commercial scale, try out a small batch first at the local farmers' market.

What you're doing is demonstrating you can sell your goods or services at that price. If your business needs outside finance then your business plan may have to show you've done your market testing in this way.

DISCOUNTING AND MONEY OFF

This can be awkward. Some ruthless people have a policy of absolutely no discounts for anyone at any time, arguing that an upfront approach like that saves embarrassing negotiations and is at least fair all around. But done correctly, discounting can be a valuable way of keeping existing customers happy and at the same time drumming up new business. Whatever you decide, you have to be consistent. Don't discount for one family member and not another. It's best to come up with a policy before you start trading and then stick to it.

Whether to offer discounts will depend a lot on the type of venture you're going into. These are some of the options:

- **Open with discounts**. The first 20 customers in your shop get 50 per cent off.

- **Fixed discounts for repeat business**. If, for example, you run a personalised guided walking company, offer a five per cent discount to returning customers. Accommodation providers can do the same.

- **Customer loyalty**. Do you supply hanging baskets, bulbs or plant stocks to the same customers, month after month? Again, offer them a discount or perhaps money-off vouchers if they spend over a certain amount each season.

♦ **Loyalty cards**. It worked a dream for Tesco and it can work for you. This is something that needs a bit of thought, so if you're starting out at the very beginning it may not be at the top of your priority list.

♦ **Encourage existing customers to help you find new ones**. Reward them with a discount, money-off vouchers or something free.

♦ **Haggling**. Force yourself to overcome that British loathing of haggling because encouraging it is good for business. If you sell your handmade garden seats with a 30 per cent mark-up then you have scope to cut the price.

♦ **Use haggling to make other sales**. Sell them the garden seat with 15 per cent knocked off and throw in a couple of hanging lanterns at five per cent below their marked price. You know what your break-even is (the customer won't) and as long as you stay within it you're making a profit.

♦ **End of day sell-offs**. If you're selling perishables (bread, fresh cream sponges) or are at a one-day craft or Christmas fair or farmers' market, you may want to sell off stock cheaply rather than throw it away or take it home again. This is a more difficult decision. On the one hand any sale is better than no sale, but on the other you don't want to encourage customers to hang around like vultures waiting for the cut prices.

♦ **Sales**, end of season or otherwise. It's such a devalued word now, thanks to year round 'sales' on the high street, that it's debatable whether they're ever worth it.

♦ **Customer credit**. It's probably best to avoid this if possible. There may be a few instances where it's good business practice to be seen to be trusting your customers to settle their bills weekly or monthly. Perhaps the goodwill generated on something like a home grocery/deli delivery service would outweigh the risk of some customers not paying. On the whole though it's probably safer and potentially less embarrassing for bills to be settled as they're incurred.

Once again it's all about balance. Sales and discounts attract business and consumers do expect them. But equally you probably don't want to become known as the discount warehouse king. It's better to sell five items at 25 per cent profit rather than 20 items at five per cent profit. In other words, think profit rather than turnover.

SALES FORECASTS

Sales forecasts sound like something only engineering or double-glazing companies should be doing. Not true: sales forecasts are equally valuable to the reflexologist, home baker or wood turner. Forecasts help you manage your business by making sure you are as prepared as you can be. This probably sounds boring and unnecessary, especially if you're going into a creative market (will you even be reading this chapter?). But nothing is more irritating than losing sales because you don't have enough stock or running out of money when a few months previously you had some spare.

Forecasts help you predict the likely patterns of your business, which means you should find it easier to:

- ensure smooth cash flow
- ensure you always have enough stock or goods
- ensure you never run out of time
- or if you do, give you time to find a helper or assistant

- identify any future problems.

Many existing businesses draw up a sales forecast once a year. Brand new businesses usually do one before they start trading. If you are writing a business plan, then a projected sales forecast is a non-negotiable element. Any would-be backer, mentor or adviser won't take you seriously without one.

A sales forecast may sound like one huge amount of guesswork, but if you've done your market research thoroughly and have checked what your competitors are up to, it should end up being more accurate than you ever thought possible.

There are lots of ways of doing a forecast. What's important is that the forecast is clear, relevant to your business and preferably put together on a computer spreadsheet. A spreadsheet, used properly, does all the adding up for you, puts everything in date or any other order you want, is easy to correct and can be updated constantly. If you can't use spreadsheets it's definitely worth taking a few hours to learn. Ask a friend, look on the internet, buy a book or go to an evening class. If desperate, you could do a forecast by hand on graph paper or use a manual typewriter, but it'll be much harder work and will look amateurish.

Where to start
It helps if you first break everything down into categories.

- **Customers**. How many do you think you'll have when you start trading? Presumably you'll have one or two, at least, lined up in advance. How many customers would you realistically hope to have after one month, six months and a year?

- **Return custom**. Depending on your product or skill, would you expect these customers to buy from you only once, weekly, monthly, annually?

- **Sales**. How much are your customers likely to spend per visit?

- **Monthly sales**. Are any times of the year likely to be busier than others?

- **Lost customers**. Realistically, how many customers do you expect to lose a year? It could be because your product or service isn't right for them or because they may be tempted elsewhere.

If you start thinking of a sales forecast in the abstract, it'll be a meaningless jumble of figures. But once you start answering specific questions relevant to your business, it will begin to make more sense.

Example One: selling vegetables

An organic veg box provider has five customers lined up before he starts trading. Through word-of-mouth and local newspaper advertising he expects those five customers to grow to seven after the first month, to 25 after six months and about 50 after a year. The box scheme is offered weekly and costs £6 per box. At Christmas, half the customers order larger boxes at a cost of £9 per box. Our box provider guesses he'll lose ten per cent of customers a year because they'll drift back to supermarkets or move away.

His sales forecast could look like this:

	Customers	£6 per box per wk	Monthly total (four wk months)
Jan	**5**	**30**	**120**
Feb	**7**	**42**	**168**
Mar	10	60	240
Apr	14	84	336
May	18	108	432
June	20	120	480
July	**25**	**150**	**600**
Aug	29	174	696
Sept	35	210	840
Oct	42	252	1,008
Nov	46	276	1,104
Dec	**50**	**150 (£6 boxes)**	**600**
		225 (£9 boxes)	**900**
Annual projected income:			*£7,524*

By January of Year Two our box provider has been proved right and
he's lost ten per cent of his customers. He's back down to 45
customers but has increased box prices by five per cent or 30p. And
he's confident he'll still be picking up new customers at a rate of
four or five a month. In July of Year Two he decides to introduce
two new ranges, organic beef and free range eggs. His sales forecast
for that year will look very different to the first year.

Example Two: selling soft furnishings

A soft furnisher plans to sell her cushions, scarves and gift bags at
craft fairs. At her first fair she'll be happy if she sells a couple of
scarves and some bags. By her sixth fair (in about three months),
her presentation and selling technique should be better and she's
expecting to sell several cushions and many more scarves and bags.
By the end of the summer she hopes to be much better at picking
fairs that suit her products. And if all goes well, by the end of the
year and in time for the Christmas rush, she's also hoping to start
selling the more expensive quilted or fake fur throws for beds and
sofas. Her sales forecast could look like this:

	Cushions £20	Scarves £10	Gift bags £5	Throws £100	Monthly total
Jan		**20**	**25**		**45**
Feb	60	100	45		205
Mar	**140**	**120**	**65**		**325**
Apr	180	150	80		410
May	200	140	70		410
June	180	120	60		360
July	140	80	40		260
Aug	140	60	35		235
Sept	200	100	65		365
Oct	**220**	**110**	**80**	**100**	**510**
Nov	220	190	110	200	720
Dec	260	220	155	500	1,135

Annual projected income: £4,980

The sales forecast turns out to be quite accurate. By the start of Year Two our soft furnisher is beginning to realise that she can make almost as much money in the three months in the run-up to Christmas as she can in the rest of the year combined. So she's probably far better off using the summer months to refine her designs and make more cushions, scarves, bags and throws to sell in the lucrative autumn and winter months. And she's added another couple of lines, mittens and linen laundry bags. Or our soft furnisher could think about widening her product range to include items which would sell well in spring and summer, perhaps sarongs and lightweight shawls.

Either way, in the meantime a couple of local independent shops have agreed to take her scarves. They sell well, and by the beginning of Year Three she's decided that her next big goal is to open her own small shop, perhaps in Year Five or Six, and maybe even expand into upholstery.

And our soft furnisher is continuing to do her annual sales forecasts, making sure the business is continuing to show steady growth; that she has enough stock at the right time of year to meet demand; and that she spends her cash wisely throughout the year, even though the bulk of her income is increasingly coming from just three or four months in the autumn and pre-Christmas rush.

Future sales forecasts

Your first sales forecast will be drawn up before you start trading. Subsequent ones should be drawn up towards the end of your trading year so you have as many actual sales as possible to base your figures on.

Forecasts for later years will become more sophisticated as you build on the early data by adding new factors. Thoughts for Year Two and beyond:

- **Customers**. Are you likely to keep your existing customers? Will those customers spend about the same, less or more with you?

- **New ranges**. Are you thinking about including new ranges, perhaps a new treatment, pottery range or line of furniture?

- **Existing ranges**. Do you expect to still be selling the same products or skills throughout the year? Do you already suspect (having done your research) that there may be less demand for some, maybe because it's freely available elsewhere or perhaps because it's too expensive?

- **Taking on staff**. Yes, you'll have to pay them, but will you recoup that money and earn more in increased sales?

- **Advertising**. Do you expect there to be increased demand every time you place an advert in your local paper? Does it follow that it will be quieter between the adverts?

- **Prices**. Do you expect to keep your prices steady for the next year? If not, what will be the impact of (presumably) higher prices? Do you think a ten per cent rise in prices will mean a five per cent drop in customers?

- **Outside economic influences**. Are interest rates likely to rise which would make your borrowing more expensive? Rate rises could also mean a reduced demand for luxury goods or services which are traditionally the first to go when people need to save money. Or is a recession looming?

- **Other outside influences**. The previous summer was a wash-out so are you expecting fewer tourists to stay at home this summer which means fewer bookings for your holiday cottage or tailored walking holiday company? Has there been another food scare that will impact on your catering business?

Alternative sales forecast method

The other way to do a sales forecast or plan is to think of how much money you'd like to make in your first year and then work backwards in trying to achieve it. In other words: 'I'd like to make £10,000 profit in my first year, therefore I need X number of customers a month who each spend Y amount on Z products or services.' In practice this doesn't work unless you're lucky and just happened to have plucked the right figure out of thin air.

The plan of action

If you're feeling conscientious then you could draw up a sales plan based on your forecast. Most of it should be obvious, but if your business is likely to be complicated or if you're keen on lists then it may help. As an example, let's go back to our soft furnisher who's fairly sure she will sell most of her cold-weather and gift-oriented products in the autumn and the run-up to Christmas. So her 12-month plan could be:

January–March:	Sell off last year's leftover stock at a discount. Consider what needs changing for the coming season. Source new materials. Produce limited stock for Easter.
Easter:	Identify early season craft fairs and sell lightweight products.
Spring/summer:	Make products for autumn and winter stock. Investigate potential new fairs and seek deals with shops. Build own website.
September–December:	Sell madly in craft fairs and Christmas markets.

SALES FORECASTS: THE EASY MISTAKES TO MAKE

◆ **Being too optimistic**. This is forecasting what you hope to sell rather than what you probably will.

◆ **Being completely wrong**. Remember that there are physical limitations to what you can achieve. A tree surgeon can only visit so many sites in a day or a food producer bottle a maximum number of chutneys or relishes.

◆ **Forecasting sales to reach your break-even point**. Tempting but pointless.

- **Having no faith in your own sales forecast**. This means ignoring the common sense on the spreadsheet in front of you, which spells out when the busy and quiet times of the year are likely to be and when you're probably going to be making the bulk of your money.

- **Not showing it to someone**. It's vital you show your forecast to either a business adviser or someone who has business experience. They may well pick up on something you missed.

CASHFLOW FORECASTS

Cashflow forecasts will show you where you're likely to be spending – useful especially in the early days when you'll feel like a human cash dispenser, spewing out money with little clear idea of where it's supposed to be going. And later on, when the projected figures become reality, a cashflow forecast will provide a clear picture of the rate of growth of your business.

Despite what the books and experts tell you, you only need to do a cashflow forecast if you're likely to have a lot of money moving through your business via many transactions, and it's important that you keep track of it. Note *money* moving through, not profit. So if you're opening a medium-sized organic restaurant where you're likely to have many suppliers, customers and money passing in and out continuously, there's a strong argument for doing one. But if you're starting out on a small scale business where your turnover (revenue from sales) is likely to be low or where you're likely to have few customer transactions, there's little point. In other words, if you're keeping a couple of ornamental sheep to knit from their wool or setting up as a hill-walking guide, don't bother.

A basic cashflow forecast

INCOME	Jan		Feb		Mar		TOTAL	
	F/c*	Act*	F/c	Act	F/c	Act	F/c	Act
Restaurant sales	900	750	1,200	1,100	2,200	2,500	**4,300**	**4,350**
Takeaway sales	200	150						
Frozen meal sales	200	200						
Wine sales	400	500						
TOTAL	**1,700**	**1,600**	**2,000**	**1,800**	**3,000**	**3,500**		
EXPENDITURE								
Raw materials	350	400						
Wages	500	500						
Heating, lighting	200	250						
Phone	80	80						
Advertising	100	50						
Insurance	100	100						
Loan interest	250	250						
TOTAL	**1,580**	**1,630**	**1,650**	**1,700**	**2,000**	**1,800**		
Surplus (or deficit)	120	(30)	350	100	1,000	1,700		
Carried f/w		(30)		70		1,770		1,770

* F/c = forecast spending
*Act = actually spent

When putting together your forecast, fill out the monthly forecast columns in advance of either the start of trading or before the beginning of your financial year. And as the year progresses, enter the figure for what you actually achieved.

It means that at a glance you can tell:

◆ If you are doing as well as you think you should be.
◆ If you are on target to make a profit.
◆ How well or how badly individual lines or segments are doing.

- If your costs are under control.
- If you can afford to spend a little more on advertising or promotions.
- If it's worth spending more on raw materials to produce more things to sell.

This isn't just a paper exercise because once you've worked out your monthly figures, you need to tie that in with whatever you've got in the bank.

PROFIT AND LOSS FORECAST

This forecast uses data from a sales forecast and a cashflow forecast and comes up with a single figure that represents what your annual income is projected to be. It takes the money you expect to earn from sales and deducts all your costs to arrive at that sum. If you haven't done a cashflow forecast it doesn't matter because you'll presumably be keeping a running total of your likely expenditure, so you can use that.

At its simplest, a profit and loss forecast could look like this:

Financial year: 2004–05

Income for year:	£20,000
Less running costs:	£5,000
Less capital allowances:	£5,000
Gross profit before tax:	*£10,000*

There's more on profit and loss accounts and capital allowances, plus balance sheets, in Chapter 14.

7

How to Create Your Business

WHAT'S IN A NAME?

Your business's name and the image it projects are important. The few words used in the name will speak volumes: is it traditional, contemporary, clever, straightforward, exclusive, to-the-point, abstract, memorable, recognisable?

When you build an image you usually only have one chance to get it right because images tend to stick. Remember the jewellery chain Ratner, forever associated with the word 'crap' after a famous speech by its own boss? Or Marks and Spencer, which shows, for different reasons, how powerful a lasting image or branding can be. Despite its well-publicised ups and downs in the last few years, it's still on the whole known for quality and reliability.

There are a few occasions when your business doesn't need a name or strong branding, perhaps because you're planning a low key business where you have enough captive customers lined up and are unlikely to need anymore. This could be if you're providing a gardening or child care service just for the families who live in your hamlet, or when you know that all the bread and cakes you can make will be sold through one or two local bakeries. In these circumstances a name, image and snazzy logo could even be counter-productive, seen as too slick and a waste of money.

But for most businesses, the name, image and branding that goes with it make up one of the key steps to success, so it's worth spending some time thinking about it.

THINKING UP YOUR NAME

You could decide on a name that identifies with your local area. This can work well, whether you're selling locally or further afield, something like Devon Creamy Yoghurts or Cumbrian Woodcrafts. Or consider an abstract name, something that conveys a business philosophy, a bright new beginning, a way of life. The Post Office famously changed its name to Consignia but it was greeted with widespread ridicule and was eventually dropped. The old British Steel became Corus after a merger, but that name stuck. Names like these don't actually mean anything, but the branding people who dreamt them up must have decided they conveyed the right corporate image.

Thinking up names is a knack and it's something you either have or you haven't. It's not something you learn. If you're stuck, find a friend or family member who's good at competition slogans and get them to have a go. And if that still doesn't produce anything then name the business after yourself. Plenty of others do.

When you've decided on your name:

◆ Make sure no one else is using the name already. It's important that you don't infringe their copyright or trademark if they've registered the name. Check with Companies House (www.companieshouse.gov.uk).

◆ Then check the internet and your local phone book. If someone nearby is already trading under that name then think up another. If they're 300 miles away then it's less of a problem. What is important is that the customer can distinguish between you, and that you can't be accused of plagiarising the name of the other business, masquerading as them or trying to poach their trade.

◆ Check to make sure the name is available as a website address. Do a Google search on 'domain names' to find someone to register it for you. (See Chapter 11 on setting up your own website.)

Other points to bear in mind:

◆ You can't use offensive names.

◆ The name of a limited company or limited liability partnership must be registered at Companies House.

◆ It can't be the same as another registered at Companies House.

◆ There are restrictions on using words like 'Royal'.

CASE STUDY: THE CORNISH SPECIALITY PRESERVE MAKERS

Tony and Sarah Marsland regularly tour France, Spain and Portugal looking for inspiration for the jams, marmalades, jellies and mustards they sell under the label Cornish Meadow Preserves. Lemon and lavender marmalade, chilli jelly and pear and cinnamon jam are some of their mouth-watering recipes.

How did it start?

We'd been living in France but wanted to return to Cornwall and needed a business to start. We'd made jams before in a small way so it seemed a logical thing to do.

Where did you sell?

We started in 1995, doing every tiny fair and school fete. We had jars worth about £200 and had picked and gathered almost all the fruit ourselves. We learnt as we went along. We eventually bought a luxury trailer which opened out into a huge stand and drove that everywhere.

What was your biggest problem?

We were contacted by Unilever who said they owned our trading name. We were OK on Cornish and Preserves but Meadow was theirs. We had to employ a trademark attorney. It turned out Unilever wanted Cornish Meadow for a new product. Eventually we signed a bit of paper saying we'd never sell their new product, but it cost us £1,500.

Do you employ anyone?

No, we keeping everything in-house. No one has the same commitment as the family. Our two elder girls help when it's busy. The business will always be there for them if they want it, along with their little sister when she grows up. And we've cut back. We sold 60,000 jars one year but it had to stop. Now we go for premium quality and premium price.

What now?

We've now got a small shop in Helston, but don't get much passing trade. We've applied for planning permission to turn the front of our house into a shop because it's in a better position. We want to expand more into speciality foods.

Website: www.cornishmeadow.com
Email: sales@cornishmeadow.com

HOW TO FORMALLY SET UP THE BUSINESS

This will vary dramatically, depending on what it is you're going to do.

If you're setting up as an odd job person, and plan to spend your time mowing lawns, painting windows and fixing leaking taps, then you'll need to do very little. If, on the other hand, you'll be:

- going into partnership
- setting yourself up as a limited company
- employing people
- taking on a franchise
- taking on premises
- doing anything involving health and safety
- doing anything involving children
- doing anything involving food and drink
- doing anything which may have an environmental impact

... then you'll be filling out a lot of forms.

Sole trading

By far the quickest and easiest way to get started is as a sole trader. You wake up one morning and decide to start selling cut flowers from the bottom of your garden. That's it: you're now a sole trader.

The key points here are that:

- Sole traders are personally responsible for any losses the business makes.

- If you can't pay your debts, your own possessions and home could be at risk.

- You should keep a proper record of your business's income and expenditure.

- Even if you're a sole trader, you can still employ people.

You need to tell the Inland Revenue which will send you a couple of simple forms to complete, confirming when you started trading. It'll then use the information you've provided to calculate your National Insurance contributions. Otherwise, the only other real thing to do is to make sure you fill out an annual tax return which the Inland Revenue will now begin sending you.

It may be tempting to start trading without telling anyone at all and work only for cash. Remember though that the Revenue runs a national team of determined and dogged staff and it also receives regular tip-offs from the public, so it'll probably catch up with you in the end.

Partnership
Going into business with a partner or partners means you'll probably have more money to invest in the business. You share the risk and hard work of decision making but you also share any profits.

The key points here include:

- The partners share personal responsibility for any business debts.

- If one partner can't pay their share of the debt then the other partner becomes responsible for it.

- A partner can make decisions and enter into contracts without necessarily telling the other partner unless you write something into the partnership agreement to stop this.

◆ Once again, the Inland Revenue has to be told when trading begins.

You need a formal agreement drawn up which spells out exactly what your business's aims and objectives are. This is not the place to scrimp on money: get a solicitor who you all agree on to draw up the contract.

The world is littered with the broken friendships of people who'd gone into business together. Think very long and hard, and then think even more, if you're considering going into business with a friend. Are you prepared to risk your relationship in the pursuit of grubby profit?

Limited liability partnership

In trading terms, this is basically the same as an ordinary partnership except that your liability is limited to however much money you invest in the business. It means that if anything goes badly wrong your personal possessions and home should be safe, unless of course you used them as collateral for a loan.

But setting up this partnership is more complicated and it involves first registering and then submitting accounts to Companies House, which makes the accounts public. The partnership may also have to be audited. If you're considering this then you need to speak to a solicitor and accountant.

Limited company

You don't have to be a big firm employing hundreds to become a limited company. There's limited liability here in the same way as there is for the limited liability partnership. But limited company status is thought to convey extra gravitas, an instant sense of size, stability and permanence. It may also make it easier for the business to borrow money, and the title probably looks better on letterheads.

- Anyone can set themselves up as a limited company.

- The company has to be formally set up and registered.

- Its annual accounts must be sent to both the Inland Revenue and Companies House, where again they can be made public and anyone can read about how well or badly you're doing.

- You can raise money for the business by selling shares in it to other businesses or individuals.

- You have legal responsibilities.

- If the company fails and you haven't carried out your duties as a company director you could be liable for the debts, disqualified from acting as a director, and even sent to prison in extreme cases.

FRANCHISES

Some of the biggest names on the high street are franchises.

Essentially you pay for a licence from a company which allows you to use its name and sell its products. You have a head start because you're selling an already established product or service, plus you usually receive support and advice from the parent. You buy the franchise and the bigger the name, the higher the price generally. So you have to decide whether the benefits will outweigh the cost.

Only buy a franchise from a business with a good track record. Franchise contracts are usually detailed so get legal advice before you sign anything. There is a British Franchise Association – tel:

01491 578050 or website: www.british-franchise.org

SOCIAL ENTERPRISES

Not everyone is driven by hard cash. You may decide you want to
set up something to benefit the community, for example a bus link
with the local town or a loose co-operative of local vegetable
growers. These are known as social enterprises when the primary
aim is to benefit the community rather than make a profit, with any
surplus money being reinvested back into the business. The
government is encouraging them because it believes they drive up
productivity and competitiveness, help deliver more public services
and result in a more inclusive society.

At the time of writing, a social enterprise still has to be structured
along standard company lines, and you need to talk to a business
adviser or your accountant about your best options if you are thinking
about setting one up. There are plans to introduce a category called a
Community Interest Company or CIC from July 2005, though this
may date may slip. According to the DTI's website: 'CICs will be a
new type of company ... easy to set up, with all the flexibility and
certainty of the company form, but with some special features to
ensure they are working for the benefit of the community'.

For more information go to: www.dti.gov.uk/cics/.

RULES AND REGULATIONS

While you're thinking about the legalities of setting up your
business there are a couple of other things to take into account at
the planning stage.

Health and safety

This is something you have to take seriously. As the owner of a business you have a duty of care to any employees, outside contractors, visitors or members of the public who may be affected by your work. You can be prosecuted for failing in that duty and in extreme cases can be sent to prison. You need to know how and when to carry out risk assessments. If you're working in an area where health and safety is likely to be a big issue consider going on a course or employ a health and safety consultant. Depending on the nature of your business you may have to register with the Health and Safety Executive. Check the HSE website: www.hse.gov.uk or call its helpline 08701 545500.

Disability access

If you're planning to open a shop, studio, workshop or other premises where members of the public may go, you need to think at the planning stage about disability access. You have to make sure disabled people can access the goods and services your business offers. You mustn't discriminate against them or any disabled employee. You need to make 'reasonable adjustments' if necessary. For example, you may have to provide a ramp to allow wheelchair access up steps to your shop, or allow guide dogs into your shop when usually dogs would be banned. In practice the 'adjustments' are what most humane people would do anyway.

8

Working From Home –
The Best Option?

Some rural businesses will mean you have to find premises, especially if you're planning any sort of shop or other retail outlet. If you're offering a service, anything from a manicure to a dry stone wall, then the chances are you'll travel to see your client. Otherwise you have the option of working from home. It could be a spare bedroom, study, converted garage or barn, or shed at the bottom of the garden.

There are three big advantages to working from home:

- There are no long, expensive commuter journeys.
- You won't have to pay for a lease or rent.

- Working from home allows you to start small and take on premises later if the business justifies it.

But there are three big disadvantages too:

- There's no escape. It's more difficult to leave work behind you, physically and emotionally, if your office is upstairs or at the bottom of the garden.

- Suppliers and customers who know you work from home will phone in the evenings and at weekends.

- Family and friends will not see your office as a work environment. They'll spread toys around, play games on your PC and come and moan to you because you're a captive audience and always there.

ARE YOU READY FOR IT?

Many people work well from home, settling into a routine and able to overcome distractions, everything from neighbours popping in for a chat to a crying child or a boiler repairman. For others it's a total disaster. These are the people who can't concentrate or motivate themselves easily and find they need the discipline of an office environment.

Unless you've worked from home before you probably won't know which camp you fall into until you start. So before you commit yourself, some questions to think about:

- Are you disciplined and self-motivated or will you spend your days drinking tea and forcing the dog out for another walk?

- Are you independent and self-reliant?

◆ Can you think for yourself?

◆ Are you good at managing your own time or do you need someone to tell you what to do next?

◆ Do you prefer working in a structured environment?

◆ Will you miss office life, the gossip and the adrenalin rush when things go well?

◆ Will you get lonely?

◆ Do you need to bounce ideas off colleagues?

◆ Are you interested in new skills and able to pick them up quickly? A successful homeworker has to be flexible and able to turn their hand to most things.

◆ How are you technically? If you've previously only worked for companies that have in-house IT support teams, what are you going to do when your computer crashes, as it inevitably will?

THE PRACTICALITIES

If you've passed those emotional tests there are then the practicalities to think about:

◆ Do you have a spare room in your home, garage, garden shed or barn which can easily be turned into your work area?

◆ If so, does it have enough space for you to work, store your products or raw materials, and keep your paperwork in?

◆ If the room doesn't have them already, is it easy to install extra phone and fax lines and power points to accommodate a computer, printer, scanner, fax and phone?

◆ Is it far enough away from your family's living area to escape from noise and small children?

♦ Is the natural light good enough (especially important for tailors, artists and designers)?

♦ Are you going to be generating noise which could upset neighbours? Craftspeople's tools and heavy duty sewing machines could be a particular problem.

♦ Are you able to easily move stock and equipment around? It's not ideal if your furniture workshop is at the top of a narrow flight of cottage steps.

♦ What's road access like? Will customers and suppliers be able to find you? Will they be able to park? Is increased traffic going to be a problem?

YOUR WORK SPACE

Working at the kitchen table is only a short term option. Soon you'll get bored with getting everything out and then clearing it away again. Food and drink will be spilled across business letters and you'll find the remains of last night's supper congealing under your laptop. And after a while, as your business begins to grow, you'll need somewhere to keep files, paperwork and receipts.

Think of converting a room and buying equipment as an investment in your future and not as a cost which will eat into your profits. A separate room also has the very obvious advantage of having a door to shut which should keep family out and allow you to symbolically leave work firmly behind you every evening. A separate phone and fax line should also help maintain a distinction between work and family life. You probably want to answer your business line professionally and not allow your five-year-old to get to it first.

HOW TO STAY SANE

Everyone works differently and your hours may be decided by the school run anyway. But consider the following:

◆ Try to start and finish at a set hour. Or have an unbreakable rule: 'I will never work past 7pm'.

◆ Have two (or three or four) breaks a day.

◆ Make sure you still see people. This is particularly important if you live alone. Make a point of meeting a supplier, customer or client every week or two. It's also good for business because it puts faces to names.

◆ Develop more friends socially because you won't have work colleagues to fall back on.

◆ Treat work as seriously as you would if you were going out to work. Tell your family and friends that your piano practice or potting up of baby bamboos is just as important as sitting in an office staring at a screen.

◆ Set yourself targets and give yourself treats if you meet them. 'If I finish this project by Wednesday lunchtime I can go for a walk/ have a bar of chocolate.' You need self discipline for this one.

◆ Ignore housework. If you were working in a formal office environment you wouldn't pop home to unload the dishwasher or do some ironing, so why should this be any different?

Housework can be an issue, especially if your partner goes out to work. This is something to resolve right at the beginning, with you making it clear that just because your work space *happens* to be in your home it doesn't mean that you automatically take on all the cooking, cleaning and childcare. How would you share the duties if both of you worked away from home? That should be your position at the opening of negotiations.

It's important not to underestimate the demands of doing any sort of work from home. Some jobs will mean that once you've physically started you've got to continue to the end – baking, pottery or joinery for example. Maintaining your train of thought is critical too. It isn't an effective use of your time if you constantly have to cross between work-work and house-work, so don't commit yourself to anything until you're sure you can cope.

Switching off

Ultimately, a successful homeworker has to learn to switch off. Many report that this is one of their biggest single problems. There always seems to be one last little job to do before going to bed, one last call to return, one last email to send, one final invoice to get out. No matter how much you love your job, you need to be able to escape from it, and taking a step back is good for business anyway because it allows clearer thought. It's all about not blurring the distinction between work and home – even though they both happen in the same place.

CASE STUDY: THE SHROPSHIRE LIVERY PROVIDER

Farmer's wife Veronica Shilton, who already had a small son and part-time job, probably would never have chosen to go into business. But in 1998, when her husband fell ill, she discovered unpaid bills, debts of almost £200,000, and their farm business in Shropshire close to bankruptcy, so she had to do something fast. Leaving wasn't an option because selling up wouldn't have covered their debts, and they had nowhere to go anyway. So Veronica, a keen horsewoman, started a livery business.

Did you have many options?

No. The cows had to go. I already had a couple of liveries to support my eventing so it was a natural progression. But in the beginning it was very hard: I was working until 2am each day. I knew about horses but had no business experience.

Could you use the existing farm buildings?

The buildings were for cows and not satisfactory for horses, but we had no money to convert anything and obviously couldn't borrow. So I did one at a time: one formal livery paid for a bit of conversion, and so on.

What do you do exactly?

I provide stables and grazing for other people's horses. I also offer full care, including grooming, arranging vets, feeding, turning the horses out in the morning and bringing them back into the stables in the evening. I look after about 30 horses on average and don't want to get much bigger. But I am expanding into horse transport, both nationally and internationally, usually to France or Germany.

Are you back on your feet yet?

This year the debts have finally been cleared, I'm due to turn over about £180,000, and should make a small profit. I always had confidence in the business but not much confidence in myself.

Yew Tree Livery and Horse Transport
Website: www.horsetransport.uk.net
Tel: 01952 460607

PERMISSIONS

If you do decide to work from home you have to be careful you don't infringe any planning conditions, leases or restrictive covenants. It's important to check because if you do break any conditions the implications could be serious.

Much will depend on the nature of your business. If you're an illustrator of children's books and work quietly at the kitchen table then it's not going to be a problem because no one's ever going to know. If on the other hand you turn your cottage into a big restaurant and takeaway then it's going to be rather obvious.

Many local authorities take a dim view of people running businesses from their homes, especially if it increases traffic or noise. This could be customers, suppliers delivering raw materials, or even extra trips you have to make in order to move stock or your finished product around. If you think this could be the case, speak to your local authority at an early stage to decide on the best way forward.

INSURANCE

If you're going to work from home you'll also need to check your insurance policy. Don't give your insurance company the chance to wriggle out of any claim, which it could do if you don't tell it about a change of use. Non-disclosure is one of the main reasons why claims are refused. It's far safer to be honest and upfront about your business activities and change your insurance cover if necessary.

There are policies designed for homeworkers. Any high street broker should be able to help, or do an internet search. You may be able to bolt on a business element to your existing household policy.

If so, it will probably add about £130 a year to your annual insurance bill. If you have lots of expensive computer equipment it could be closer to an extra £300. Shop around though: some insurers recognise that homeworkers are a good bet because the property is occupied more often (less chance of burglary and fire) and adjust premiums to reflect that. If you have specialist tools or equipment you may need a more tailored policy. If you travel and take business equipment with you, such as a green energy consultant's laptop or a landscaper's tools, you need to make sure the policy includes those risks. Most professional and trade associations offer beneficial rates to their members.

Other risks to cover

As well as standard buildings and contents cover, plus business equipment in and away from the home, there are other risks you need cover for.

◆ **Business interruption**. If your home burns down, where are you going to work from? A good policy will cover you for a temporary office or studio, plus the cost of moving. Sometimes it's included as standard and sometimes you may have to pay extra.

◆ **Public liability**. Vital if you'll have any business visitors to your home. Again, sometimes it's standard and sometimes you'll have to pay extra.

◆ **Employer's liability**. You'll need this if you employ any staff.

COUNCIL TAX AND BUSINESS RATES

If you're working from home, there's a thin line between when you should pay council tax and when you may have to pay business rates. If it's still your home, and you're only using one room, then you may end up paying both. This isn't necessarily a disaster because business rates aren't always higher than council tax.

The Valuation Office Agency (VOA) is the section of the Inland Revenue which deals with council tax and business rates in England and Wales. In Scotland it's Scottish Assessors. (From April 2005 the Valuation Office will be an executive agency of Her Majesty's Revenue and Customs. The Inland Revenue and HM Customs and Excise are merging.)

This is what its website says:

> *If you work at or from home, you should be aware that the accommodation within your home used as an 'office' may be liable to business rates whilst the remainder of the property will continue to be liable to council tax (although an alteration may be made to its banding).*

> *There are many considerations that we must make in deciding whether a room in a house used as an office should be liable to business rates and each case is considered on its own merits. We will consider the effect of the extent and frequency of the non-domestic use of the room and any modifications made to the property to accommodate that use.*

It goes on to say that a VOA member of staff will usually visit the property before an assessment is made. The website gives examples of how different cases could be judged.

Example One
A detached Edwardian dwelling in a residential area owned and occupied by a self employed solicitor who practices from the property, specialising in Matrimonial Law. The front room on the

ground floor is furnished with sofa and comfortable chairs, has a TV set, and ornaments/photos of a personal nature displayed around the room. It is used on an occasional basis as a waiting room for clients during week days, and as the lounge by the occupier during evenings and weekends.

The former dining room is used as an office equipped with computer, dedicated fax and telephone line, filing cabinets, desk and shelving stocked with law books. No domestic use is made of this room. It is used by a part-time secretary when the solicitor is visiting clients or attending Court. The ground floor kitchen is used for preparation of family meals, but also to make tea or coffee for clients. The first floor accommodation of bedroom and bathroom is wholly used for domestic purposes.

The VOA's assessment

The office is the only non-domestic part and will be assessed for business rates. The principal purpose of the front room is to serve as a lounge. In this instance, the non domestic use is sufficiently minimal so as not to warrant assessment for business rates. The lounge and the remainder of the dwelling will be banded for council tax purposes.

Example Two

An integral garage of an estate house is converted to an office with plastered walls, electric power points, solid front, suspended ceiling and floor screed suitable for carpeting. A separate telephone line has been installed. Access is through the hallway of the house. All toilet facilities are in the main house.

The occupier claims that the room is used by the family in the evenings and occasionally at weekends. During the day the occupier designs computer software. He is employed by a major company to work at home, because of a physical disability. All of the equipment has been provided by his company and is specially adapted for his needs. He visits his former office on an occasional basis.

The VOA's assessment
The former garage is no longer domestic property. It has been adapted for office use and should be assessed for business rates. The remainder is domestic.

Example Three
The occupier is employed as a site finder by a major building company, and travels across most of the southern part of the country, using her home as a base, but calling into the company office once a week to pick up new instructions, for meetings, and to leave completed work.

She has a 4 drawer cabinet in the corner of a dining room, which also functions as an 'office' for the family computer, and there is no dedicated telephone line for business purposes. The occupier is out visiting sites 4 days a week, and does 'writing up' at home on the dining room table in the evenings and at weekends. No clients or members of the public visit the house for business purposes.

The VOA's assessment
The whole of the dwelling is domestic property, and should be banded for council tax.

The website address is: www.voa.gov.uk/council_tax/ working_from_home.htm

Another government-funded site has been set up, designed to put everything the small business ratepayer may need to know about rates and valuation in one place. Working from home is covered too. The address is: www.mybusinessrates.gov.uk.

Information on the site is for ratepayers in England only. Ratepayers in Wales, Scotland and Northern Ireland should talk to their central or local authority.

MORTGAGE TENANCY AGREEMENTS

It's possible you could break the terms of your mortgage, or tenancy agreement if you're renting, if you run some types of business from home. Check with your lender or landlord if you think this may be a problem.

OTHER WEBSITES

There are many other sites devoted to working from home. Many offer practical tips: others concentrate more on lifestyle. In most cases, get onto the site and do a local search on working from home. Some of the sites have case studies of homeworkers which are worth reading for the tips they give.

www.egrindstone.co.uk

This site downloads quickly, it's good looking and professional and there's plenty there.

www.homeworking.com

A site for anyone working from home, including the employed who work remotely away from the office. The site is fast and well-designed.

www.ivillage.co.uk

This site is aimed squarely at women, but there's lots of good material on it which is relevant to anyone working from home. The site is slow to download and the layout is a bit fussy.

www.startups.co.uk

This is thorough, packed with everything you'd ever need to know about the practicalities of working from home, but rather dull.

www.businesslink.gov.uk

This site is aimed more towards the employer and employee working remotely from home rather than the freelance, but there's still plenty of detail here.

www.wfh.co.uk/wfh/index.htm and **www.workingfromhome.co.uk/ wfh**

These are basically sites set up by British Telecom to sell you all the gizmos you'll need. Useful perhaps if you need equipment to get started, but shop around.

9

Spreading the Word: How to Advertise

If you're selling goods or a service in the countryside, by far and away the best method of advertising is word of mouth. First, it's free and second, people are more likely to believe it. But word of mouth works both ways. If whatever you're selling isn't very good, too expensive, is late arriving or doesn't do what it's supposed to, then word will get around just as fast.

Word of mouth advertising is fine if it happens. But other than giving your customers a good service and hoping they'll tell family, friends and neighbours, there's not much else you can do to encourage it. So you'll almost certainly need other methods of promotion or advertising.

Advertising is all about striking a balance between how much you spend and what you get back in return. Unless you're lucky (or very clever), it's going to be trial and error until you establish what works for you. In the first year or two be prepared to make mistakes and waste money. In later years, even when you're more experienced and have learned where to spend the money to get the best responses, you are going to have to keep refining your approach because nothing is ever constant.

Either way, brace yourself to spend some money to spread the word because few businesses can get away with doing absolutely no promotional work at all. Don't think of an advertising budget as eating away into your profit, even though it does. Try instead to remember the hackneyed but still true cliché: you've got to speculate to accumulate.

MAKING YOUR NAME VISIBLE

A lot of advertising is about product or name recognition. Your potential customers won't need whatever it is you're selling all the time. Instead, what you want to do is to make sure that it's your name they remember when they do eventually come to buy.

There are endless ways of raising your profile, and think of it as a positive tick in a box every time someone hears or sees your company name. So consider:

- **A sign-written van**. Every time you get in and drive down the road your company name is being seen by a lot of people.

- **Carrier bags and packaging**. Why do shops always put your tiniest purchase in a bag? Because it turns you into a walking advert for them which has cost them virtually nothing.

- **Key rings, pens, sticky notes, calendars**. All excellent ways of subliminally getting your name around. These types of items tend to hang around for months.

- **Telephone answering machine message**. Every time someone phones you, even if it's a wrong number, they hear your name.

- **Letter heads and compliment slips**. Every time you write to someone, send out an invoice or respond to a query, your company name and logo is there at the top of the page.

- **Business cards**. Scatter them everywhere but make sure they're good quality. Nothing looks worse than an amateur design on cheap cardboard. Don't try to cram too much information onto them.

- *Yellow Pages*. Everyone uses these. Some businesses report the majority of their custom comes this way. It helps if you fall into an obvious category because it makes you easy to find.

- **Thomson local directories**. Also worth being included in.

- **Give a talk**. Organisations like local WIs are often keen for new and interesting guests to come and talk to members. Many meetings are well attended, and talking to 30 or 40 people in a different community every month is a fabulous marketing opportunity.

- **Sponsorship**. Think about who your likely customers are going to be and where you're most likely to catch their attention. If you are a wine merchant, sponsor a menu or a table in your local bistro. Landscaper? Pay for a prominent local verge and do something eye-catching.

- **Promotional events**. These are most successful for anyone working with food or drink. Wine merchants can hold wine tastings, deli owners can do the same with cheese or olives. It's trickier to know what to do if you're a blacksmith or dry stone waller.

- ◆ **Christmas cards**. Send out lots and send them out early. The earlier the cards arrive, the more likely the recipients are to read them. You'll also save by sending them second class. If you're a designer or have access to one, then create your own cards because they'll be more memorable.

- ◆ **Networking**. A toe-curling word, but don't let that put you off because networking works. Get out there and meet people. Talk to them, be nice to them, ask them questions about themselves, find out what they can do for you and you for them, make links and associations between different groups.

BEING MEMORABLE

Think up a company name and stick to it. It doesn't have to be clever or alliterative, but short and snappy is best. There's absolutely nothing wrong in using your own name. Get on your computer and find a typeface that you like, and again stick to it. Think too about the use of colour. What image are you trying to get across? Businesslike (sober black), environmentally sound (green!), arty (anything really). A logo isn't obligatory. Unless one is screamingly obvious (a tree for tree surgeon) then it may be best to leave it. If you're not a designer, a home-grown logo can look awful and amateurish, and that's not an ideal image to project.

When you've decided on your name, typeface, colour and design, show it to as many family, friends and acquaintances as possible and get their honest opinion. When you're satisfied, plaster it over everything – delivery vans, letter heads, bags and so on.

And remember the two golden rules:

1. Keep it simple.
2. Keep it the same.

TARGETED ADVERTISING

A lot here will depend on your type of product or service and who your customers will be. Are you likely to be selling to the whole community (bakery, gardening, shoe repairs) or to a much smaller section (dry stone walls, website design, bespoke jewellery)?

Local newspapers

Many communities have thriving local newspapers. On the whole, the daily papers are likely to be regional, cover larger areas and will be more expensive to advertise in. For our purposes, the weekly papers are likely to be a better bet. First, they'll be cheaper; second, they hang around for a week so people are more likely to see your advert; third, they're local and you'll target your own community more accurately; and fourth, there's a great tradition of local papers carrying small adverts, and many are sold on ads rather than news content.

Local newspaper advertising is suitable if your product or service is likely to appeal to the whole community. Don't waste your money on this if you're providing something specialised, whether it's an unusual product or service or something outrageously expensive.

If you want to splash out and take a boxed advert, remember that white spaces stand out on a page and not words. Don't be tempted to cram in too much detail: less is usually more, so grab their attention and then provide them with enough detail to take it forward, either a phone number, website or shop address, craft fair date and location, whatever.

Generally, the more adverts you take out the cheaper it becomes. Discounts are usually offered over a period of time, such as a month, a quarter, six monthly or annually.

Leaflet drops

These can be effective if you're targeting a smallish area and you're confident that most people receiving the leaflets will at least be interested in whatever it is you're offering. If you're a jobbing gardener and live in a village with a high percentage of elderly and/or working people, then leafleting can be extremely effective. The same is true of a bakery or grocery round in a remote area miles from the nearest shop or private language lessons in the catchment area of a school with a famously bad languages department.

But don't waste your time and money if you're not confident that your product or service is going to be relevant to the local community. This is especially true if you're selling through a website and will probably be posting your product to customers. What's the point? Remember that producing an A5 leaflet needn't cost very much (you can do them yourself on your computer), but delivering to hundreds or thousands of houses is both time consuming and boring.

Local radio and TV advertising

This is always an option if you're aiming high. Yes, you'll reach a lot more people (and you'll pay for it), but are they likely to be the right sort? Younger people listen to independent local radio so no point advertising your home crochet service there, while local TV advertising is the ultimate scattergun approach. It's seen by everyone, but is that what you want? Should you be aiming more at your specific target customer?

Specialist publications

These are much more useful if you're offering something a bit different. Perhaps you're a restorer of antique weapons or offer bed and breakfast accommodation aimed mostly at walkers and bird watchers. Identify the magazines and periodicals that those type of people read and spend your money there.

CASE STUDY: THE CAMBRIDGESHIRE ORGANIC WHEAT PRODUCER

The organic wheat grown on Glebe Farm at Huntingdon in Cambridgeshire is milled, bagged up and sold for bread machines, hand baking and as bread mixes. The business started in 2001 with just a few bags sold at farmers' markets: production is now up to two and a half tonnes a month and is sold to health food shops and delis across the UK, with other outlets in Jersey and Gibralter. Turnover is about £60,000 a year. The company's run by Rebecca Rayner, who took over the 1,500 acre family farm six years ago when she was just 27.

What was your previous experience?

I have an agriculture-related degree. I worked in sales for an agricultural feed company, then joined a management training programme. And of course I grew up on the farm.

How did you get started?

When I took over the farm I knew we had to do something more, and it was an easy transition to this. We had the wheat, the space and a lot of the basic equipment already, and I gradually invested more as the business grew. It's all been self-financing, no grants.

What's next?

Our flour has just been accepted by Waitrose for two of its local stores. We've started in the gluten-free market and already it's one of our strongest lines so we want to expand there. It's all about adding value to the basic product.

Any tips to pass on?

Test the market first. You get great feedback free from farmers' markets which would costs thousands from focus groups. I'll continue to do farmers' markets to test new lines. And don't spend lots of money on new equipment because there's plenty of second-hand out there.

Glebe Farm Organic Flour
Website: www.glebe-organics-flour.com
Tel/Fax: 01487 773282

PREPARING PROMOTIONAL LITERATURE

Most businesses benefit from having some sort of brochure or promotional leaflets. They have two main purposes:

- to catch the attention of potential customers
- to convey information.

Leaflets, or flyers, are usually the simplest form, taking a single sheet of A4 or A5. The leaflets can be stuffed through people's doors, tucked into bags of shopping at point of sale, left on shop counters, included when sending out invoices or answering letters of inquiry, or inserted into other material which is being distributed (local papers and magazines). Leaflets should include some detail, but not all. A brief description of your product or service, a picture or illustration and where it and/or you can be found, is enough.

Brochures are the place to include the full detail, so list and illustrate everything you do, adding prices, availability, delivery terms, shop opening or appointment times, and anything else relevant to you.

For both brochures and leaflets, it's vital that you:

- Think about what you want to say to your customers or clients. What message are you trying to get across?

- Consider your image. Solid, reliable, traditional, innovative, imaginative, exclusive, creative?

- Use decent quality paper. Cheap paper says cheap product. It doesn't have to be gloss. Anybody providing a traditional service or goods may prefer the parchment type.

◆ Get your literature professionally designed. Anybody can type out a list of products and prices but that's not going to sell anything. An imaginative, well thought out and relevant brochure will. This is worth spending money on. For some businesses this is imperative, usually at the high value end.

If you're competent on a computer and have an eye for design, you can do much of the work yourself. Otherwise get the professionals in to design and print the material for you. This sort of mini-desktop publishing is competitive, with plenty of people offering these services, so it probably won't cost as much as you think, somewhere between £250 and £500. Usually, the larger your print run the better value it is relatively.

HOW MUCH TO SPEND ON ADVERTISING

It's usual to spend about five per cent of your gross income or turnover on advertising and marketing over the course of a year. This isn't very helpful if you're just starting out and don't have any income at all to base your budget on. So the next best thing is to go back to your business plan and use the figures in your cashflow and sales forecasts. In any event, you're unlikely to spend your whole marketing and advertising budget in one lump, so if you're unsure, then spend a bit where you think it's most likely to be effective and sit back and see what happens.

You'll find it useful if you can come up with a system of finding out where your new customers are coming from. That way you can evaluate whether you're spending money in the right places. If they just walk in off the street with no nudging, then forget about marketing and spend your money on stock or new tools. But if they're responding to leaflets or local paper ads then you know you're on the right track.

Every business is different and you may find you have to spend much more, perhaps up to 12 or 15 per cent of turnover, especially in the first year or two, in order to get launched.

NEWS RELEASES AND HOW TO WRITE THEM

The best way of all is to get publicity that doesn't cost you anything. If you can persuade a journalist to write a story about you or feature your business in any way, then this is ideal. Not only is it free, but it should be more credible because you haven't paid for its inclusion.

But don't send off a lengthy description of your bread-round business or revolutionary new method of growing tomatoes and get affronted when they don't print it word for word. Newsrooms are swamped by news releases, and most of them are far too long, muddled and boring. On the whole, you have to find a new angle for something to be newsworthy.

- Have you genuinely come up with something new and interesting?

- Are you creating jobs for locals?

- Have you brought in Californians to teach at your surfing school?

- Have you secured a spectacular order (sold noodles to the Chinese or wood to the Finns)?

- Have you had a record production run (made ten times as many Christmas cakes as last year and sold them all by the end of November)?

- Have you just moved to new and unusual premises (making children's Halloween costumes in the local castle dungeons)?

News releases shouldn't be any longer than a single side of A4 paper, with double spaced typing. Start with a big heading at the top (journalists, simple souls, need to know what it's about, and quickly). The opening sentence will determine whether the reader will continue or throw the release in the bin, so keep it short and to the point. If you've written a 100-word opener, then get rid of it. Get someone to ask you *out loud* what the story is, and nine times out of ten your reply will be your opening sentence. Then take two or three brief paragraphs to elaborate. End with your contact details. If appropriate, attach a photograph.

JOE BLOGGS GARLIC FARM

Date

Little Hambling farm sells garlic to the French

Little Hambling farmer Joe Bloggs has won a quarter of a million pound order to sell his fresh Hampshire garlic to French supermarkets. Joe won the order after meeting the supermarkets' agent at a trade show. His previous biggest order had been for £75 to supply the two grocery stores in Greater Hambling.

Joe has two more months to bring on the bulbs before he can start sending stocks over. He has to take on three extra staff to meet demand and expects to be working an 18-hour day himself for much of the summer.

Joe said: 'The garlic I grow is different to the type usually found in France, which is why they were interested. I knew the agent would be at the trade show, so we brought some bulbs along to show him. I also cooked some in a Spanish omelette and gave it to him to taste. He loved it!

'Selling garlic to the French is only the beginning. I'm expanding into onions and I'm hoping they may be interested in those too. After that, I may try garlic soup, garlic relish, even garlic jam and jelly.'

Contact: Joe Bloggs
01234 ... (Farm)
01234 ... (Home)
07777 ... (Mobile)
Email: joebloggs ...
Website: www.joebloggs ...

Standing out from the crowd

It's all about getting your news release to stand out from everyone else's. Having a good or interesting story to tell helps, but it's not always enough. Journalists are snowed under with offers of news items. Releases pour in on email and with every post, publicists phone, freelance agencies offer tip-offs, websites are updated every second. Remember that your little item of news is in direct competition and jostling for space with all these things plus, depending on the medium, national and international news, politics, business, sport, accidents and disasters, the environment, health, crime, cuddly animals, multiple births ...

So what else can you do to make your release stand out from the crowd? Journalists (like everyone else) love something free. Are you a food producer? Attach a small box containing a (hygienically) wrapped chocolate truffle, cherry tomato, slice of walnut bread, whatever. Better still if you have a vineyard and can send a tiny mouthful sized bottle of your latest wine. Make accessories? Then parcel up a pair of evening gloves, costume earrings or dress ring. You can never guarantee you'll get some free news coverage out of it, but your news release is more likely to get to the top of the pile and read first.

But think hard about offering anything more substantial as an inducement. Few journalists can guarantee coverage because the final decision is usually up to their editor. A week in your seaside guesthouse or the gift of a hand-carved chair could add up to quite a lot of money, as well as looking a bit too much like a big fat bribe.

If the release gets used

If you're lucky, you may get a follow-up call. If this happens, be prepared to be interviewed. Despite what you may think, journalists are rarely out to get you. Almost all want a quiet life, so listen to the questions they ask and answer briefly and relevantly (an astonishing number of people go off on wild tangents, talk for hours, then are amazed when the piece never gets used). Be pleasant and helpful, and you'll almost certainly be treated likewise in return. Radio and TV interviews are more nerve-wracking, but if the interviewer is any good they should make you feel at your ease once things get underway. In any case, think of it as a conversation rather than as a formal interview.

Afterwards be prepared for three things:

◆ Only a fraction of what you've said will get used. This isn't personal: space is usually tight, especially on radio and TV (when viewers and listeners have the attention span of a gnat anyway).

◆ Inevitably you will think they've got some facts wrong. Sometimes journalists get things wrong, especially if they're in a hurry. Sometimes you will be misunderstood. Sometimes there is more than one way of looking at something. Sometimes things get rewritten and edited by a third party. Only complain if something is so seriously wrong that it will severely damage your business, and you can prove it.

◆ The angle or slant may well be different from what you were expecting. This is more likely to happen if the journalist is going off to interview someone after you who may offer a different view. Well it's tough. There's no point in asking for approval of the item before it's published because you won't get it. So you either have to trust the journalist or never send out a news release.

Building up a relationship with the media
This is the ideal. If at all possible, and you think you're personally

suited to it, try to establish yourself as a local spokesperson in your field. If you're a tree surgeon or landscaper could you always be the first person the local media talk to when they need a comment about logging or the latest arboreal disease? Are you an organic producer, happy to discuss the wider implications of pesticides or cheap imports? Or a picture restorer, able to put into context the discovery of an old master in an attic in the next village?

Again, it's all down to name recognition. The more your potential customers are aware of you, your name and what you do, then the more likely they are to use you. Remember the old saying: all publicity is good publicity. On the other hand, you don't want to be thought of as the local rent-a-quote ...

THE LAUNCH!

This is the best marketing tool of all, so don't hold back. It's your big opportunity to get your name around and tell everyone what you're up to. Hold a big party and invite everyone you think could be even remotely useful to your business. Dream up a stunt relevant to whatever it is you're selling. Painting landscapes? Then send them up in hot air balloons. Anything in catering? Then themed, slap-up food, colour it all blue, say it's from Burma or all grown in matchboxes ... whatever. Anything to be remembered. Then send them home, oozing goodwill, with a gift bag of decent goodies (not cheap key rings or calendars).

Hold the launch party at about the time you start trading.

10

How and Where to Sell

There's no point in having the best product or service around if you don't sell it in the right way. You can't afford to sit back and expect your customers to pick up telepathically what a brilliant job you've done. Instead you have to stick it under their noses and present it in such a way that whatever's on offer is immediately better and more enticing than those of your competitors.

THE ART OF SELLING

Some people are natural sellers, most of us work hard at it and get there in the end, and then there's the minority who read every self-help book on the planet but are still terrible at it. Hopefully you'll be one of the first two, but don't despair if selling really isn't your thing. What is important is to acknowledge it early on and either get a partner who can, or sell through an agent or other third party like a wholesaler.

But you never know until you try, so give it a go at least once or twice. There are a few simple rules to remember:

- Listen to your customers and take your cue from them.
- Do you sense they want to talk or be left alone?
- Don't gabble out of nervousness.
- Smile and stay relaxed.
- Be patient.
- But persevere (gently) if you think they're wavering.
- Don't point score.
- Know everything there is to know about your product or service and be prepared to answer questions.
- But don't be too clever.
- Be confident.
- Be polite but not oily.
- Be yourself.
- Be aware of body language. If their body is closed to you and they're backing towards the door, you know you've overdone it.
- Know when to stop.

The point of sale is also a good opportunity to let your customer know if you're doing anything else they may be interested in. Perhaps if you're a landscaper you may have a sideline in selling organic vegetables, or if you're an aromatherapist can you either sell your own oils or recommend a good source?

REPEAT BUSINESS
Once you've made a sale, it's far easier to make another sale to the same person. They know your product or service and can trust it.

People on the whole are conservative and will usually go with something familiar. Perhaps the customer liked your product packaging, ethical approach or attention to detail. Ask them what it was that appealed to them. It's also cheaper to sell products to existing customers because you know they're out there. It means you don't have to spend so much money on advertising or other promotions.

There's something called the 80:20 rule which says that successful businesses need to get about 80 per cent of their income from 20 per cent of their client base. What this means is that you need to create a core of loyal customers who'll return again and again with little prompting, giving you time to concentrate on finding new customers and refining your product or service.

But of course you don't want to neglect the loyal core. If possible, keep contact details for them. Let them know about new lines, tell them first about sales, discounts or special offers. Make them feel valued.

SELLING AT CRAFT FAIRS AND MARKETS

Selling at fairs and markets rather than shops is slightly different. There tend to be fewer barriers between sellers and customers, the atmosphere more relaxed and informal, and customers more likely to want to chat. There can also be a festive air or sense of occasion if the fair or market is held at Christmas or at an annual agricultural show or village fete. So be prepared to get into the spirit of things and think about how you can make best use of it.

Selling at fairs and markets can also be more personal. Usually you're selling your own goods, often handmade, which says a lot about you as an individual. Contrast that with a typical shop which almost always sells factory-made products from many sources, which are sold by assistants who don't care if the goods have been made by Indian slave labour or dropped from the heavens.

All the usual rules of selling apply at fairs and markets, but because it can be more relaxed you need to be a bit careful. Remember that there are still boundaries.

- Don't be too familiar.
- Don't be too pushy. Don't jump out from behind your stall the moment customers approach because they'll take off like a nervous deer.
- Don't take rejection of your products personally.

Remember too that not everyone is the same and that you'll have to develop different approaches for different situations. Think about how you would sell your product or service to, for example, an elderly farmer, a well-to-do middle-aged woman in a Barbour jacket, or a young mother towing a couple of children. Then practise on patient family and friends.

A good selling technique is something that only comes with experience. Don't get downhearted if you find it difficult or even distasteful at first. As your experience grows, then so will your confidence and skill. And consider the advantages of starting out at a fair or market:

- There should be many more passing customers than in a shop so you'll have plenty of chance to practise your selling.
- There'll be a greater cross-section of people.

◆ You get instant feedback on your product or service.

◆ You can pick up ideas from other traders, both in how to sell and in how to display goods.

And you can learn all those skills without having to commit to a shop or studio.

HOW CRAFT FAIRS WORK

How to find them
Small fairs and fetes are everywhere you look, in village halls, schools and community centres. They're almost always run by someone local so it's easy to track down the organiser. Once you get in the loop, you'll hear about other and larger fairs and markets through your fellow traders. Specialist fairs and markets are advertised through dedicated magazines and websites.

How to get in
It's easy with the very small fairs: usually they're pleased to take anyone they can get. In the medium sized events, try to get your application in early. Preference is usually given to businesses who've sold there before so you may have to go on a waiting list. The really big events are more difficult. You usually have to submit a written application and portfolio of your work to show you're a serious and deserving trader who'll add something to the occasion.

Cost
Fairs can be reasonably cheap to enter, about £50 for a small local fair, but rising to hundreds or even thousands for the big events lasting weeks. If you join something like a craft guild which has a big presence at a show you can sometimes get reduced entry charges.

Even if you don't sell very much at first fairs, shows and markets are still excellent advertising opportunities, so it's probably still worth going along anyway. Make sure your trading name is prominently displayed on your stall so as many people as possible see it.

Setting out your shop front

It's standard to be provided with a trestle table (check dimensions in advance), a chair or two if you're lucky, and access to electricity, so take an extension cable.

Your stall is your shop front, and its appearance and layout is what's going to determine whether you sell a few pounds' worth or shift the lot. At the beginning, until you learn what works for you, it's best to:

- Keep a plain, dark, neutral background. A black or navy blue cotton throw will be fine.

- Add height around the sides and at the back. Use stout shoe boxes and solid lumps of wood of varying depths. Once they're covered, no-one will know what's underneath.

- Use lighting. Even in the summer, unless the room or hall is particularly bright, a well-lit stall will look more inviting and eye-catching. Wind a string of discreet small lights around your products, perhaps train a couple of spotlights to highlight something you're particularly proud of, or just use a side lamp or two to add ambience.

- Don't display anything low down at the front or out-of-sight because it may get stolen.

Customers like to touch and handle things so make it easy for them to do so. If your product is soft, fluffy and tactile (teddy bears, chiffon scarves), pile them up in low baskets and put them right at the front of your stall. If it's scented candles or soap you're selling, leave some unwrapped for people to sniff.

Rows of jars of pickles and chutneys can be brightened up by scattering among them the raw ingredients you've used. So bring along bowls of fat red chillis, strings of onion and garlic, and packets of spices like star anise, nutmeg and turmeric to add perfume, colour and general exoticism.

If possible, offer tastings because people will feel more obligation to buy. If you want to offer tastings of alcohol, check with the event's organisers beforehand that this is allowed.

As far as the overall look is concerned, remember that less is more. Don't pile up your product so that every last inch of surface is covered because it'll only look messy and amateurish. Play around at home with layouts and ask family, friends and neighbours what they think. At the same time, look at shop window displays and think about what works or doesn't, and why.

Think too about the packaging you're going to sell your product in. Make it part of the experience. Don't use cheap paper bags: splash out on packaging which complements your product and adds to the customer's feel-good factor. As a bonus, try to come up with something that they can use again and again, perhaps a hat or shoe box or good quality stripy paper bag. But make sure you include a small, discreet business logo to keep reminding them of your existence.

CASE STUDY: THE SCOTTISH LEATHER WORKERS

Leather working is big business in Jessica Pascoe's native Peru so it was a logical trade to pick up on when she and her British husband David moved back to the UK in 2002. They settled near Aviemore in the Scottish Highlands and started selling the handbags they make at fairs, festivals, and markets.

Did you have any previous experience?

I had a bit of business experience and Jessica had done some leather working back home in Lima so we both had to practise a lot before we started producing really good bags.

Did you do much market research?

We just made a few handbags and tried selling them. We tested the market as we went, refining the bags until we got it right. Accountants and analysts kill an idea every time. You can talk to people all you want but you've just got to try it. At first we sold purses and wallets as well, but are now concentrating on the bags because there's more profit in a £60 handbag than a £7 purse, and it takes almost as long to make a purse as it does a handbag.

How much outside help did you have?

We went on a three-day business course run by a local enterprise agency. As far as finance is concerned, we didn't need much to set up the business. It's mostly self-financing but we haven't been able to take much money out of it yet.

What's been your biggest challenge?

Finding the right places to sell. People buy handbags on impulse and tourists spend more than locals, so we've learnt that we need fairs and markets which attract plenty of visitors. The Edinburgh Festival was particularly good for us. It's taken about 18 months to feel properly established, but we're getting there now.

Machu Picchu Leather Craft
Email: PascoeLeather@aol.com

The hard work

Fairs and markets are physically hard work. Before you sell anything you have a lot of preparation to do.

* The night before, prepare, pack and stack your products.
* On the morning, load the car or van (not much fun on a bitter November day, pre-dawn).
* Put together a packed lunch and flask (you probably won't want to leave your stall).
* Drive to the venue.
* Unload the car or van and carry the goods to your spot.
* Unpack.
* Take packing cases and other packaging back to the car and park (often some way away).
* Arrange your stall, shelving and lighting.
* Display your product or service details in an enticing way.

And it's still only 8.30am. You have the whole day ahead of you, on your feet, often in an icy town hall or wind-blown farm show marquee, and you have to keep smiling.

At the end of the day, you do the whole lot in reverse. And it's considered bad form to pack up early and go home while other traders are still at it. It's probably difficult to do it practically anyway. So even if you've sold out by 2pm or you realised within the first half hour that this wasn't the event for you, tough. You're there to the bitter end.

Because you do a lot of standing around, make sure you take plenty of warm clothes. Even in summer early mornings can be chilly. In winter you'll need everything you can find, proper thick socks and gloves and a hat. Don't rule out the trusty hot water bottle either.

Identifying the best fairs and markets for you

The Holy Grail. Finding the right places for your product or service is absolutely critical. It can mean the difference between taking a couple of pounds and a few thousand. There's absolutely no point in getting into an agricultural show where the main business is in the stock ring if you only sell lavender-stuffed foot stools. Equally, if you're a jobbing tree surgeon don't waste your time on WI markets.

So two important rules:

1. Find a venue where you're reasonably sure that most of the people there are the type to be at least interested in your product or service.

2. And make sure they come to spend money. A large crowd doesn't automatically mean lots of shoppers. One trader reports that Highland Games are never good for him because the crowds are always too busy watching the events to buy his leather goods.

Shows spread out over a few days are time-effective because you only have to set up and take down once, but make sure there's decent overnight security in place.

Meeting your public

Your mum was right – first impressions do count. Strangers aren't going to recognise your inner beauty if they have to see past greasy lank hair, dirty hands and stained clothes. Dress appropriately – no one expects an artist to wear a suit or a cook to be draped in primrose chiffon – but basically neatly.

When you meet your public for the first time it can be a shock. How can anyone not want to buy your lovingly crafted product? Don't they realise how much thought, care, sweat and worry went into it? But don't get anxious or angry because it's not personal. You will have to learn to live with rejection and accept that most people will be able to get along quite happily without you.

Instead, turn every encounter to your advantage. Watch what catches the customer's eye and listen to what they say to each other. See if any particular product is better at drawing them to your stall. One accessories maker reported putting a fluffy white hopelessly impractical cushion right at the front of her display. Naturally no one bought it but they all came to stroke it, and while they were there they bought other things.

Selling other people's goods

Most craft fairs and farmers' markets expect you only to sell your own products and not goods bought in from somewhere else. But if you're determined to do this, there are ways around it:

- No one is going to mind too much if most of what you sell is your own work.

- Goods bought in from elsewhere could perhaps be labelled 'designed', 'inspired' or 'created' by you.

- Try at the very least to provide the raw materials for products that have been packaged elsewhere, for example you've grown the flowers or herbs for pot pourris.

- Or maybe you've put together your own product from other people's initial efforts, perhaps local calendars of photographs you've selected and bought in.

But if you're still determined to sell a majority of other people's work just don't flaunt it.

SELLING A SERVICE

Just because you're selling a service rather than a tangible product, it doesn't have to mean that marketing or a good display is any less important. Agricultural or country shows can be an important showcase for landscape gardeners, while portrait painters may do well at markets in the run-up to Christmas. It's a good selling point: 'Stuck for a present idea? Then give someone you love a picture of you.' This approach works best with doting parents or a love-struck partner.

Photographs and pictures

Anybody providing a visual service has a head start because the obvious thing to do is to adorn your stall with large photographs of whatever it is you do. Think well in advance about the display, what you want to get across – perhaps your precision or expertise, or use of colours or textures – and select your photos or drawings accordingly. Once again remember that generally less is more. Three or four well-chosen pictures, carefully-hung, will have a greater dramatic impact than scores of smaller ones, pinned haphazardly to a board.

Whatever you decide with the pictures, remember to think about the background. This is largely common sense: if you're displaying photos of gardens you've designed, then don't use a flowery or busy background. A plain and neutral one is far better.

Examples of your work

If you're an upholsterer or seamstress, once again display photos of your work. But also have with you examples of something you've done recently. A newly upholstered wing chair in sumptuous plum velvet is a real eye-catcher and positively invites passers-by to come across and sit down. And once they're sitting down, get them chatting and lo! you've got them hooked. Almost everyone has a tatty old chair or stool somewhere in the attic that they'd like to have re-upholstered 'one day when I get around to it'.

Other things to display

- If possible, your raw materials, perhaps swatches of fabrics or garden bulbs and seedlings.
- Free samples (see below).
- Your brochure or publicity leaflets.
- Your business card. Give them out by the bucket load because people do hang onto them.

Not forgetting yourself

Remember that for those people with a product, it's usually the product that's pushed. If you're selling a service, then it's you who's important. So don't stay behind your stall. Come out to the front and be prepared to be inspected, and chat and explain what you do. People attract other people so if you're worried about standing out there like a lemon ask a few friends along to get things moving.

It's a little more difficult if you're a ditch digger or tree surgeon. Pictures of stumps aren't great attention grabbers, so you may need to adopt a rather more businesslike approach.

SELLING AT CHRISTMAS

Throw taste to the wind and get out those gold and silver baubles. In the run-up to Christmas, even the most aloof and snooty shopper sings along to Slade and secretly loves fairy lights. And even if you personally think it's a case of 'bah humbug', well tough: get into the festive spirit or you'll lose business. Anyone producing crafts, gifts or in any way connected with catering or hospitality, should be able to make as much money in the run-up to Christmas as they can in the whole rest of the year.

Christmas displays

You don't have to turn your stall into a crazed display of cheap flashing lights and plastic Santas. Instead think about introducing tasteful sprigs of holly, red berries and pine cones, either natural or gold sprayed. Use a few good quality fairy lights. Shops like John Lewis sell large round platters, sprayed a deep matt gold, which make excellent display bowls for fabrics, foodstuffs and small boxes. Scatter tangerines and shell-on nuts around. At the front of your display fill an eye-catching bowl with Quality Street or something similar to draw in the customers. Make your stall warmer, more welcoming and enticing than anyone else's.

Christmas presents and gift packs

The closer it is to Christmas, the more desperate people become. So make it easy and label your goods accordingly. An antique lace laundry bag made by a seamstress could be labelled as a Present for Grandmothers; a selection of relishes, chutneys or fine cheeses as Presents for Anyone Who Likes Eating; or an Indian-jewelled hand mirror as a Present for Difficult Teenage Daughters.

Gift packs are clichéd but they do work. And they don't all have to be shrink-wrapped, straw-lined baskets.

♦ If you're a home knitter, tie up a pair of mittens, socks, scarf and ear muffs in a huge gold ribbon.

♦ In catering, line a hamper with good quality silver paper or a red checked gingham, add small jars of jams, rounds of cheese or hand-baked biscuits, and fill in the gaps with nuts, tangerines and small, wrapped chocolates.

♦ For a nursery man or woman (plants, not children), put together a shallow wooden crate of spring-flowering bulbs, gardening gloves, gardener's kneeler, and perhaps a subscription to a gardening magazine, secure the whole lot with twine or raffia, and top with a sprig of holly.

Stocking fillers

Try to come up with a new Christmas line that only costs a pound or two. It could be a brown paper packet of half a dozen anemone bulbs, tiny silk gift bags or a cellophane pack of three or four hand-baked chocolate chip cookies. It doesn't necessarily have to be your own products this time, but anything that will draw the customers in to you. Again, fill a large and lovely bowl with your chosen stocking filler and stick it right at the front of your stall. In the last few days before Christmas, when a lot of the bigger presents have been bought, it's often the smaller items that catch the customer's eye.

BEATING THE COMPETITION – NICELY

You may think you have nothing to fear from the man in the stall opposite who's offering a garden design service, the elderly couple next to you selling storage boxes with pictures of kittens on them, or the farmer's wife who's popped in to sell a few eggs. Not true. Every single stallholder is after the same thing as you – the customers' money. Therefore you need every advantage you can possibly get.

- ◆ If you have any choice about which stall to take (and you may not have), make sure it's on a main thoroughfare and not stuck in a corner.

- ◆ Don't get too close to a loo exit because on the way to it would-be customers have other things on their mind, and on their way back they'll sail straight past you.

- ◆ Definitely don't be too close to a loo exit if you're selling food or drink.

◆ If you're not selling food or drink, park yourself next to a stall that is. It'll be even better if they're giving away free samples of local cheeses, clotted cream, biscuits, whatever. While the customers are waiting for their food or drink, they'll be milling around in front of your products, and three quarters of the battle is getting people to stop and look in the first place.

◆ Take every inch of display space you can, so get to your pitch early to set up. Erect any extra shelving as far out as you can without aggressively invading your neighbour's territory. Think as well about extending forward by using a small table, although you're less likely to get away with this if the aisles are narrow.

It is important not to upset the other traders. There's usually a great sense of camaraderie among them, and if you decide to follow this fair/market/agricultural show route, you'll start to see the same faces cropping up after a while. You'll pick up gossip about where the best shows are and how to get into them, and you'll learn from the traders who've been selling for years. You watch each other's stalls when you go to the loo, and you have someone to talk to when business is slow.

FREE SAMPLES

Apart from standing there naked and handing out £5 notes, there's nothing to beat a free sample for attracting a customer's attention. It doesn't matter if it's curiosity or greed: those samples will get people flocking to you. Think carefully though about what to offer. It can't look too mean, but equally it can't be so generous that it bankrupts you.

◆ If you're a carpenter or woodworker, try tiny pieces of polished wood, cut for drinks' coasters or drilled for key rings, or perhaps offcuts tied with a gold ribbon for Christmas kindling.

◆ A professional cake baker has lots of options, tiny individual muffins, cheesie straws or chocolate-dipped fresh fruit (particularly tasty with strawberries).

◆ Candle-makers can use wax sheet ends to roll baby candles with miniature wicks.

TRADE FAIRS

Trade fairs are usually open to trade only, as opposed to craft fairs which sell direct to the public. Trade fairs are where you go to meet potential agents, wholesalers and other middlemen. They can be expensive to enter and it will take time to prepare your pitch. It's also more of a long-term investment because it can take months for you to start seeing the benefits. So trade fairs are not something to worry about in the early days of your business. Once you've become more established, check them out through your own suppliers, trade magazines or specialist websites.

SELLING THROUGH AGENTS

Selling through an agent can bring big benefits and big pitfalls. A good agent who knows his market can get your product into scores of shops within months. But you need to read your contract carefully, especially the section on what happens when the arrangement comes to an end. Depending on the wording, agents may be able to claim a percentage of your sales long after the contract has ended, arguing that they built you up and got you onto the shelves in the first place.

You can expect to pay an agent between 10 and 15 per cent commission on the deal. By far the best way to track down a good agent in your field is by word of mouth recommendation. Talk to fellow traders at fairs and markets and find out who they use and who they avoid.

YOUR OWN PREMISES

This is a big step and not to be taken lightly. In some cases there may be no choice and you may have to plunge in. Otherwise start slowly, using the fairs and markets to check the demand for your product or service, learn your selling and build from there. It could be an expensive mistake to sign a long lease for a shop or other premises, spend a small fortune fitting it out, and only then discover it's in the wrong place with little passing trade or no parking, or that you have simply chosen the wrong product.

SELLING THROUGH OTHER OUTLETS

A happy compromise between trudging around craft fairs and gambling on your own shop is to sell through someone else's. This could be a small independent retailer or a national chain. It's far easier to get into the former. It's just a question of knocking on doors and asking to speak to the manager. Depending on the product, it'll probably be on a sale or return basis; occasionally they'll buy stock outright. Brace yourself for the shock of how little they'll offer and how much you'll see your goods marked up by. A 100 per cent mark-up is not uncommon. You'll probably just have to accept it.

Getting into the larger stores is more difficult and you have to decide whether it's worth the hurdles they'll make you jump. You may have to agree to:

* amend the product design or recipe to suit their tastes
* let them sell your product or line exclusively
* change the label or packaging
* abide by extremely strict quality control
* be prepared to produce a lot more if the demand is there.

Think too about complementary selling. This is where two parties agree to promote each others' goods in order to increase sales. So if you're producing jars of homemade cranberry sauce, contact your local organic turkey supplier. Or landscape gardeners could recommend good sources of plants or equipment in return for prominent advertising in the suppliers' shops.

SELLING THROUGH WEBSITES
See Chapter 11 for information on setting up your own website.

As well as all the usual consumer legislation, there are some extra rules if you sell goods or services online. It's mostly common sense because it just means you have to provide customers or clients with clear and comprehensive information to help them decide whether to buy. Some of the points to include are:

- full name and contact details of your business, including an email address
- price, including all taxes
- delivery charges, if applicable
- arrangement and date for delivery of goods or services
- information about the right to cancel the order.

You should also say whether you intend to offer substitute goods if those ordered aren't available, making it clear you'll pay for postage if the goods are returned.

These rules also apply to other methods of remote or distance selling, including via the phone, mail order or fax.

For a full list of dos and don'ts, plus more business information than anyone could ever possibly want, get hold of a copy of the No-

Nonsense Guide to Government rules and regulations for setting up your business. It comes from the Business Link stable (see Chapter 5).

EBAY

The online auction house eBay is one of the great internet success stories: it's got millions of users worldwide. Not everything has to be sold by auction. Many businesses sell their goods at a fixed price, or 'Buy It Now' as eBay puts it. There's quite a bit of reading to do about how the system works, but it's easy to understand. If you decide to sell this way then buy a few things first in order to build up a customer rating. This is known as a feedback score and it underpins the eBay system. The feedback comes from customers rating each other so it's the ultimate in self-policing.

www.ebay.co.uk

Don't expect to make a fortune in your first year of trading. Don't even expect to make a profit. If you've broken even then you'll have done well. It'll take months, perhaps years, to refine your product or service, and you'll never stop learning.

11

Setting Up Your Own Website

M ost rural businesses will benefit from having some sort of presence on the internet. You can either set up your own website or join someone else's. Unless you're planning a major online trading site, it probably doesn't matter in the early days as long as you get a mention somewhere. This means that when someone does a search for your type of business, your name pops up.

DO I NEED MY OWN WEBSITE?

If you're new to this, think of a website as space you rent on the internet. It can either be a single page on the screen or as many pages as you want. You can include as much or as little detail as you want.

At its simplest, your website could include a couple of photographs, a brief product description and your contact name and phone number. At its most sophisticated, the site should include photos of all your products or services, lists of colours, fabrics, materials, ingredients, whatever is relevant, plus up-to-the-minute prices and availability. The customer can buy immediately, using their card details, or go off and have a cup of tea and think about it. The first is the equivalent to an advertising hoarding, the second is an online shop.

Websites can also be used to get valuable feedback on your business. Invite visitors to the site to leave their comments, take part in a survey or email you with comments and queries. You can also keep a running check on the number of visitors to your site.

If you're not sure if you need your own site then have a look on the internet and see what's out there already. Look at competitors' websites and other websites relevant to your trade before deciding.

If you decide you don't need your own dedicated website, or don't want the hassle of setting it up and then running it, think about joining someone else's. If for example you offer bed and breakfast accommodation, could you register on a local tourism site? If you have a shop in a small market town, does that town have its own site? If you're a specialist craftsperson, look at ways of getting onto sites that promote your particular field, whether it's jewellery, bespoke furniture, stained glass windows or wrought iron work.

QUESTIONS TO ASK YOURSELF

Don't be bullied into thinking you must have your own website. Despite what your teenage children may tell you, or what you read in the newspapers, the world will still turn if you decide not to. If you're aiming for a purely local business then there probably isn't much point. You're far better off spending your time and money on buying a new delivery van or developing better products or skills.

But if you decide in principle that you want a website then think about these points:

- The internet is global. How will you feel about taking orders from Ecuador or Oman? Are you prepared to specify on your site which countries you'll do business in?
- Are your goods easily packable? Either for a UK or a global market?
- How much would you charge for postage and packing?
- Who is going to pay? You or the customer?
- What about after-sales care? If your handwoven rug falls apart in a week and your customer lives in the next village they can easily return it. But if that customer lives at the opposite end of the UK or on the other side of Europe, what then?
- Is your product likely to need spare parts? If so, how are you going to get them to the customer quickly and simply?
- Do you have the time and money to set up your own website?
- Do you have the technical ability?
- Do you have the time and money to maintain your own website?

TO BUILD OR NOT TO BUILD

It's perfectly possible to build your own site if you're prepared to put in the time. There are scores of existing websites out there designed to help you do it. Go to a search engine (a facility that helps you find things on the internet). Google (www.google.co.uk) is one of the best. Type in the words 'build a website' and you'll find quite a bit of choice. On the day I tried (January 2005), more than 40 million separate entries came up worldwide, and more than nine million in the UK alone, so you should be able to find something to suit you.

If you do decide to build your own site you could find yourself typing in a lot of code (called HTML) which is easy to follow but can be laborious. Other options include buying a shop-in-a-box system which builds your site from a database. Or it's now possible to choose from a variety of templates which you then customise to suit your business.

If you decide to employ someone, then broadly the more complicated the website and the more it can do, the more it's going to cost you. A basic website built by a professional will cost from about £1,000, though if you can find a competent teenage geek working in a bedroom you can probably halve that. If you want to make your own changes to the site, for example to update price lists and availability, this will probably cost about £500 more. If you decide on an all-singing all-dancing site with flashing logos, pop-up boxes, music, graphics and interactive facilities, the cost will run into several thousand pounds. You also need to budget to spend about £200 a year on running costs, which will mostly go to the host (the company that actually puts your site on the internet).

Even if you settle on a basic website, you can't just get it set up and never look at it again. You have to make sure it's up-to-date because nothing looks sloppier than a two-year-old price list or out-of-date phone number. You also need to change the content of the site every now and then in order to maintain customer interest. Visitors to the site will get bored and won't return if it looks the same month after month. So change the photographs, include news about you and your business, personalise it, make it relevant to the seasons, anything really to make it an interesting site that visitors will want to return to.

CASE STUDY: THE OXFORDSHIRE WIND FARM DEVELOPER

Nigel Goodhew passionately believes in renewable energy. He's a director of RidgeWind, a company based in the small village of Lyneham near Chipping Norton in Oxfordshire. It finds sites which may be suitable for wind turbines, leases the land from the landowner, usually a farmer, and then develops and builds the wind farms.

How long has the company been running?

We started in March 2003. We have three sites going through planning at the moment, one near Scunthorpe, one on the Scottish east coast near Brechin and another on the west coast. There's another five in the pipeline and about another fives sites that are looking good. They're scattered across the country which is a good hedge.

How did you get into it?

I was a grain trader for 20 years which involved a lot of 5.30am starts. I literally wanted to change my life. A family friend, Margie Glasgow from Houston in Texas, who's now company MD, had business experience and major success in the energy sector and was investigating wind farms in the UK. I was looking at renewables and could offer landowner contacts, so we got together.

Did you need much backing?

RidgeWind has two large American companies backing it, one of which is a group set up and run by Margie. We also have joint ventures with other parties. Into these deals we bring our land contacts and capital.

What about public opinion?

You can't be arrogant and insensitive. Any new industry is going to be thoroughly scrutinized and rightly so. We don't consider potentially controversial sites. The planning process is there to weed out the inappropriate sites anyway.

RidgeWind
Email: ngoodhew@ridgewind.com

INTERNET VERSUS CONVENTIONAL ADVERTISING

You have to think about how much of your business is likely to come via the internet. If you guess it could be the bulk, then you should be spending most of your advertising or marketing budget on setting up a really good site and making sure it has good links to other relevant sites. This is particularly likely if you're planning to work in anything tourism related, such as bed and breakfast accommodation, because many people now research their holidays entirely online. If on the other hand your business is likely to come from more local sources, then save your money and spend it closer to home where it'll have more effect.

THE DESIGN

Regardless of whether you employ a professional to design your website, you should still have some ideas about the overall look and content. Draft something first, keeping at the back of your mind what you want to get across.

Is the website meant to be:

◆ an advertising platform
◆ or a fully functioning online shop?

Then think about:

◆ What you want on the front page.

◆ What sections or pages you want (products, price list, about the business, about you, map to find you, and so on).

◆ What photographs, illustrations or graphics you want to use.

◆ Whether you want to include pop-up boxes or music.

- How it's all to be laid out.

- How you're going to part people from their money. Make sure the section which takes orders is particularly easy to find and easy to order from.

- What fonts you like (think about the image you're hoping to get across – traditional, contemporary, funky).

- What colours you like.

Generally the front page is where visitors first enter your site so think of it as your shop window. And like any shop window, it has to grab attention and entice people to enter. Unless you're being deliberately obscure, an obvious map or overview of the site is always welcome. And make it easy for your customers to speak to you. Put your phone number and other relevant contact details at the bottom of each page. Yes the internet is a world-changing invention, but many people still want to speak to a human before they buy.

Other points to consider:

- Adding your own pictures is easy. Either use a digital camera to take your own or copy and paste material you've found on the internet, but be careful about copyright.

- Think about copyrighting your own unique logo or other branding mark.

- Make sure your site is designed in such a way that customers see terms and conditions or disclaimers before placing an order.

A website designer can advise you on all these points. If you use one, at least go in with a couple of ideas of your own.

COMMON MISTAKES

Big isn't always the best: some of the worst websites are those of the largest and most powerful companies. They've probably spent tens of thousands of pounds on website design and the results can be awful.

Common mistakes include:

♦ Far too many photographs or graphics, especially on the front page. They take too long to download and the customer gets bored and goes off and looks at something else.

♦ No explanation of what the company actually does. That's fine if you're Manchester United and the whole world knows you play football. Otherwise include a sentence or two; it doesn't have to be a book. Something like 'Lancashire's largest supplier of boat hooks' or 'The only kipper smoker west of Argyle' is fine.

♦ No obvious way into the site.

♦ Badly named navigation buttons.

♦ No obvious address or telephone number (is this often deliberate?).

♦ FAQs (frequently asked questions) or help guides which are of absolutely no help at all. Get a trusted customer to write this section.

♦ Infrequent updating (price lists from 2002).

♦ Pages that are inexplicably not available.

♦ Boring text.

♦ Text written in jargon.

An easy way to check if the site is user-friendly is to ask an internet novice to try to navigate their way around it.

LINKS TO OTHER SITES

No website should be an island. Many sites are linked by the click of a mouse. The link should benefit both parties. Perhaps, if you're that bed and breakfast provider, you may have reciprocal links with your local tourist board. Or if you run an organic bakery, you could have a link to the website of your local provider of organic fruit and veg.

TAKING PAYMENT OVER THE INTERNET

You have two basic choices: set up a credit card facility on your business bank account or sign up with one of the online payment handling companies. These companies can securely receive, process and send on transactions on your behalf.

Which method and organisation to use will depend on the volume of business you expect to do online and the level of charges levied. Have a look at something like www.worldpay.co.uk or www.paypal.co.uk

SECURITY

Think about the level of security you need on your website. There are the payment transactions. Some business may ask customers for sensitive information. You may want to set up a whole secure area of your site for registered users only, which would be password protected.

MONITORING VISITORS

You want to know how people are using your site, whether they're new or returning visitors, which pages they look at and for how long. It's basically the same as counting the number of visitors to your shop or stall. Once you've got the information you can use it to improve your site and therefore increase business. The collection of this data is known as traffic reporting. If you want to include it then it needs to be thought about at the design stage.

Be aware of the Data Protection Act. If you'll be collecting data from and about your site visitors, you need to make it obvious to them that you're doing so. Depending on what you intend to do with the information, they should have a chance to refuse. Check your own obligations under the Act.

DOMAIN NAMES

All websites have unique names, known as domain names. Allocation of names is on a first-come first-served basis, so even if you've formally registered your business name with Companies House or anyone else, that doesn't guarantee you'll get the internet name to go with it. It's probably best to think up a name that you like, then check that it's available, both for a business and a website.

If you can't get a domain name identical or similar to your business, then think of something relevant, short, memorable and easy to type in. You can combine any letters and numbers for your name (as long as it's lower case and the numbers are between 0 and 9), but if it's too long or too complicated, there'll be a lot of typing mistakes and no one will ever find your site.

Famously, so the story goes, someone beat the AA (the vehicle rescue people, not the drinkers) to www.aa.co.uk. It had to make do with the next best thing which was www.theaa.co.uk

Be extremely careful that your domain name isn't close to a name that triggers a porn site. This is far easier to do than you'd believe because the most unexpected names have been highjacked by the porn merchants in order to lure innocent visitors to their sites. So when you've thought of your address, and checked that it's available, sit down and type in variations on your address (as if you were making typing mistakes) and see what comes up.

Don't bother registering a near identical name or logo to one of the big boys in order to benefit from their fame. First, many large companies will already have registered close variations on their name to avoid that happening, and second, just because it's the internet and not the real paper world, it doesn't mean their lawyers are any less sharp.

There is some choice in the ending of the domain name.

- **.co.uk** is the most usual
- **.com** if you're feeling global or plan to lay the foundations of a multi-national corporation
- **.biz** is for businesses
- **.org** for non-profit-making organisations
- **.info** for information services.

And there are other options. But on the whole people expect the **.co.uk** ending, there'll be fewer typing mistakes, so it's probably best to stick with that.

REGISTERING THE DOMAIN NAME

Do a Google (or similar) search on 'domain name' and scores of companies will pop up who'll be able to register your domain name for you, assuming it's available. These companies are basically brokers or middlemen who register your name with the European body which administers the definitive list of names and makes sure there are no duplications. Many of the companies offer to host your site for you as well. You can register names for up to ten years, but will probably have to renew it every couple of years. It's not expensive: basic packages are offered from just under £10.

HOW TO FIND A WEBSITE DESIGNER

None of this you'll have to do yourself if you decide to use a web designer. Most designers will put together your site and if you want, host it, maintain and upgrade it, and sometimes market it. If you decide you want them to do everything, they'll probably offer you a monthly or a year-long contract. It's probably better to sign up to a monthly contract which allows you the flexibility to change. On the other hand, you may have complete confidence in your designer and will have other things to worry about, especially in the early months of trading, so a year-long contract may suit you personally.

When picking your designer, ask to see other websites they've designed. Ask too for references. If possible it's always best to find someone via word of mouth recommendation. If you're down to plucking names at random from the *Yellow Pages*, try at least to find a designer who seems to understand what your business is about and the image and vision you have for it.

Check carefully on the technical support they're offering. If your business is going to be heavily dependent on the website and it crashes, this is as devastating as a shop burning down. You won't be doing any business until it's rebuilt.

Make sure the contract between you and the designer assigns all copyright to you.

WEBSITE PUBLICITY

Pushing your website name is as important as pushing the name of your business. Make sure the website address is on all your letter heads, business cards and other business correspondence. Email internet and computer magazines inviting them to review your website. Email any specialist publications that cover your field and tell them about the website. Build up a list of customers to regularly email with news and updates on your website: encourage them to sign up friends to receive the regular email.

But make sure you have something interesting to say every month or quarter. Designers can talk about their new jewellery lines for the coming season, florists about their plans for Christmas bouquets, but dry stone wallers or tree surgeons could find it a little trickier to maintain an interesting supply of news.

12

Bartering

There's one way of selling that's been around for probably thousands of years. It doesn't involve shops, websites, money, packaging or even a company name. All you need is a product or service that someone else wants, and who has something to offer in return. It's called bartering.

Bartering is not the preserve of some old hippies stuck in a 1960s time warp, swapping eggs for hand knitted socks or cabbages for leather thong bracelets. Instead, in the last couple of decades, bartering has been re-invented and is now seen as a valuable selling mechanism, both for businesses starting out and for those already established.

Local Exchange Trading Schemes, or LETS, provide a framework for members to exchange skills or goods without money changing hands. There is a nominated unit of 'currency', usually named locally. Provide someone with a product or service and you are credited with X units of this currency. When you want to buy something, you use the credits you have in the 'bank'.

A WAY OF LIFE

As an added bonus, LETS schemes help create a sense of community among members and bring together people from different backgrounds. Some groups go further still, and see bartering as a way of creating harmony in a community, where members can fulfil a genuine desire to help others. They consider it more of a philosophy, a statement about how we should be living our lives, rather than just a crude mechanism to swap goods or services.

A member whose account is in credit is identified as someone who's given more 'favours' than they've received, while a debit account identifies a member who's taken more 'favours' than they've given, so far. Neither situation is a problem because a debit/credit situation is necessary to make the system work. Instead, it demonstrates the principle of give-and-take between LETS members.

WHAT CAN BE BARTERED

Virtually anything can be bartered, as long as one party offers and another has the need.

Specific skills or professions:

- plumbing
- car or bike repairs
- legal advice
- book keeping

- shiatsu.

General odd jobs:

- ironing
- gardening
- babysitting
- chopping wood
- dog walking.

Something to offer:

- a van for hire
- tall ladders
- lifts to shops/work/school
- muscle power to move large furniture.

Goods to sell:

- clothes
- home grown fruit and vegetables
- homemade food such as bread, cakes, jams and chutneys
- crafts such as leather goods, jewellery, pottery.

HOW THE LETS SYSTEM WORKS

There are variations, but essentially members are given a 'cheque book' and a list of members, along with what they have to offer. If you want a product or skill, you contact the member and negotiate a price in LETS. When the transaction has taken place, the book keeper or administrator of the scheme credits the LETS to the right account. LETS are not usually physical tokens.

The unit of currency doesn't have to be called a LET: there are regional variations. For example, the currency of the North East Dartmoor LETS scheme is called the Tin (tin used to be mined locally). The name is also a play on the name of the local River Teign. Some LETS schemes break down their currencies into smaller units. The currency in the Forest of Dean in Gloucestershire is called the Dean, which is subdivided into Vicars.

New members' accounts start at zero. When members leave, they're expected to close their account at zero or in credit. Most LETS schemes allow members to become overdrawn on their credits, within reason, because if someone is spending a unit then it means another member is earning them. No interest is usually paid on LETS accounts.

The currency's value

But what is a unit of LETS currency actually worth in real money? Or is it even necessary to fix an exchange rate? It probably is worth establishing a guide, if only to give members a starting point for negotiating a price. Many schemes seem to end up thinking of a unit of their currency as equal to about £1. Some recommend an hourly rate, again as a starting point to negotiate. This tends to be in the five to ten unit range.

In practice, pricing in LETS is more fluid than in the world of hard cash. Negotiations are carried out between individuals and there's rarely a take-it-or-leave-it price. If the price being asked for clearing an overgrown allotment is too high, perhaps it'll seem more reasonable if the provider also digs over the ground and clears a few sickly boundary trees. Because of these negotiations, there tends to be a far wider range of pricing than you would usually expect to find.

Membership

Most LETS schemes are cheap to join, charging only enough to cover costs which usually have to be paid for in sterling, such as postage and printing. North East Dartmoor charges up to about £5 to join, depending on your income. For that, you receive a LETS directory, cheque book and regular updates. The renewal is £3 a year, payable in sterling or Tins.

Schemes generally seem to have between 50 and 150 active members. North East Dartmoor has 120 trading members, and a larger group of about 250 loose members who have passed through the system since it began in the early 1990s.

The book keeper

One member is nominated to keep records. When there's a transaction, a receipt or 'cheque' is issued and the book keeper receives a copy and enters it, usually on a computer spreadsheet or similar. The book keeper sends out regular statements to members, usually monthly. In the North East Dartmoor scheme, lists are posted in the local courtyard café which is used by members. Many schemes post public lists of activity because it:

◆ demonstrates to current members how active the system is
◆ encourages new members to join.

Keeping in touch

Almost all LETS associations meet regularly and publish newsletters, keeping members up to date with what's on offer, who's left the scheme and who's joined.

Many also hold trading days a few times a year where members trade goods and services between themselves. They're also seen as recruitment drives to bring in more members of the local community.

POLICING THE SYSTEM

LETS schemes are run on trust. Self-regulation usually works because in rural communities, where the bartering system is most common, it makes absolutely no sense to fall out with fellow members who are probably your neighbours and whose children go to school with yours. Some groups have an 'overdraft' limit to stop accounts going into debit rapidly (easy for a new member to do). In these cases, the member is usually encouraged to try and reduce their debit or overdraft as soon as possible. They can widen the range of goods or services that they offer, never refuse a trade or perhaps tweak their service to meet a gap in the market.

In the North East Dartmoor scheme, there's a 500 Tins overdraft limit. Very rarely does anyone take advantage. They report that occasionally a nice letter is written to suggest ways of reducing the debt.

On the whole, LETS currencies are thief- and fraud-proof. Because the units of currency can never leave the system they have no worth in the outside world and therefore there's little point in stealing them. The currency isn't usually tangible vouchers, therefore there's nothing to counterfeit (in the unlikely event anyone would bother, just to secure a free babysitting service or regular bakery supply). It's a near perfect currency where the worst that could probably happen is that a member runs up a big deficit and leaves the area quickly.

CASE STUDY: THE DEVON TREASURE CHEST DESIGNER

Retired teacher Richard Thomas started making treasure chests from his home in Chagford in Devon six years ago when his wife, who needed one for a school project, couldn't find anything suitable in the local antique shops. Like all proper treasure chests, these have a magnificent barrelled lid with brass fittings and are lined with old maps.

Is there much demand for them?
Yes. After people saw the chest I made for my wife I had several enquiries and it grew from there. They're often bought for presents, for weddings, christenings or birthdays. When I make them on commission, I line them with maps made to look old, and the maps chart the recipient's passage through life, where they were born, grew up, met and married, whatever's relevant really.

How much do they cost?
It depends on the quality of wood and the type of handles, hinges and catches, but usually anything up to about £70. I accept cash or Tins (the North East Dartmoor LETS currency) or a combination of the two.

Where do you work from?
From a workshop attached to my home. Working with wood and with my hands has always been a hobby so I had a lot of the equipment already.

How do you sell the chests?
I advertise in local newspapers, depend on word of mouth and also sell on our LETS scheme trading days. But I don't want to get too big and become too pressurised or too busy because I'll lose the joy of making them. So I prefer to make only a few a year, usually on commission, so it doesn't become a production line. Each treasure chest is unique, and when you don't turn them out by the hundred, you can afford to spend a bit of time on them and enjoy the process.

BUSINESS OPPORTUNITIES

There's an argument that LETS systems create more business opportunities in the largely rural communities where they're based. LETS, the theory goes, adds a new tier to a local economy and generates wealth that isn't accessed through the conventional monetary system. In English, this means that even if hard cash isn't available, trade in goods and services is still possible. This in turn creates new opportunities for business expansion.

For example, you're a market gardener. You're desperate to expand your growing area but can't afford to pay anyone to clear an overgrown field and don't have time to do it yourself. You consult your LETS directory, do a deal with someone fit and healthy with time on their hands and pay them with a three months' supply of fruit and veg. Result: they cut their shopping bill and you have more produce. Everyone wins.

LETS schemes are also excellent marketing and networking tools (though some of the 'greener' members may not like to see it in such harsh capitalist terms). If there's a loose alliance of a couple of hundred members in your own scheme, and perhaps one or two other schemes operating within your county, you've automatically got an introduction and shared goodwill among a significant section of your local community. If they have a choice between getting their fruit and veg from you or from Tesco, where are they going to go?

It's also claimed that LETS schemes can make you cash richer because the more transactions you conduct through bartering the fewer pounds you need to spend. This is probably only true if you have plenty of free time. If you're turning down sterling-paid work in order to do something tradeable, then that's not cost-effective. You still have to pay the mortgage, the gas, electricity, phone, water, council tax or business rates, insurances, run the car, buy petrol ...

If you do want to use a LETS scheme to advance your business, you have to be honest and upfront about it. Offering your time in return for a regular supply of potatoes is one thing: doing it because you want to make lots of money is quite another. It's usually possible to buy or sell something using a mixture of the LETS currency and sterling, especially if part of the transaction has to be brought in from the outside (petrol, for cxample). But it's generally frowned upon to ask for sterling for the whole trade.

Multi-LETS
LETS systems have developed to such a sophisticated level that a method has emerged where a group can benefit from the scheme but doesn't have the hassle of administering it itself. A multi-LETS system is effectively an umbrella organisation which registers individual schemes and its members. The members can elect to trade in as few or as many individual schemes in the collective as they choose. The benefit is that members can have access to a far wider range of goods and skills and in return have a larger potential customer base for their own. But at the same time they can still belong to a smaller local club whose aims and objectives they're more likely to share.

International trade
LETS is now global. Have a look at this website: www.LETS-Linkup.com. It's an international LETS directory which features 1,500 like-minded schemes in 39 countries spread across all continents. It allows you to:

- travel, using the system
- trade your goods through the system.

THE GREATEST ENEMY

The greatest enemy is apathy. Every scheme starts off buzzing with energy and enthusiasm but after a few years many report that membership tails off. There seems to be two main reasons. First, there always has to be an administrator, so someone has to put in a lot of unpaid work, updating records, arranging meetings and trading days and sending out statements. And second, bartering usually involves negotiation or haggling and that's something the British still aren't very good at. It's difficult and embarrassing to pick up the phone and ask a complete stranger to mend your curtains or give you a lift to the doctor.

TIME BANKS

Time Banks neatly avoid those two problems. Banks usually employ at least one paid person who looks after all the boring paperwork and who acts as a broker or co-ordinator in deals between members. Time Banks work by valuing everyone's time equally. You give an hour and you get an hour back, no matter what level of skill is needed for delivery. It's a literal form of communism, where a dog walker's hour is valued on a par with that of a doctor or dentist.

Have a look at the website www.timebanks.co.uk. It says (December 2004) that there are 71 Time Banks up and running, with about the same again in development. More than 4,000 people are involved, who've traded more than 200,000 hours.

TAX AND INSURANCE

If you're considering trading via a LETS scheme or Time Bank you need to seek advice at the time about any tax implications.

According to the Time Bank website, there's a ruling that time credits are tax exempt and will be disregarded by the Benefits Agency. It adds that LETS scheme members have not been allowed this same benefit. You also need to speak to your insurance company if you start trading beyond the usual scope of your policy.

LETS schemes and Time Banks tend to work best with plenty of active members so it doesn't pay to be shy. Make sure all your products or skills are accurately listed in the appropriate magazine or directory, and read carefully the 'wanted' sections. Can you tweak whatever you're offering in order to do a deal? Any deal is usually better than no deal, regardless of whether it's in LETS or hard cash.

13

You've Started Trading

TRADING TIPS

- Make sure you never have to go back to a job: do it properly in the first place. *John, cabinet maker.*
- Ruthlessly drop lines that don't sell. *Sue, soft furnisher.*
- Don't have so few clients that the success of your business depends on only a couple of people. *Chris, environmental consultant.*
- Keep up to date with training. You'll lose customers if you don't know the new techniques. *Nicky, hairdresser.*
- Never give discounts to anyone. *Sarah, dinner party caterer.*
- If you're not terrified in your first year, you should be. *Phil, alternative energy provider.*
- Treat customers as you'd like to be treated. *James, garden ornaments designer.*

- Cashflow is king. *Sally, small business MD.*
- Don't be too pushy trying to make a sale. *Katherine, candle maker.*
- Count pins in and count them out. *Trevor, upholsterer.*
- In January people spend Christmas gift vouchers: you had the money months ago but now you have to give them the book. *John, book shop owner.*
- February is the worst trading month. Knock ten per cent off everything. *Pam, beautician.*

Your business is finally up and running and you've had your first few customers. It won't matter if you're launching a multinational or selling a few handmade pottery mugs you'll share the same sense of elation at having finally done it.

The first few weeks and months of trading will tell you whether:

- you've picked the right business and have plenty of customers
- you've picked the right business for you and are happy in your work
- your family is happy with your work commitment
- the business is going in the direction you hoped
- the business is likely to meet the aims you set for it at the beginning (hobby job, life support system or world domination).

You shouldn't be in a position when you start a business of having absolutely no customers and none in sight. Your business plan, market research and other preparation should have stopped you in your tracks and shown there was no demand for your product or skill long before you got to this stage. Equally, if you have plenty of customers but are working 100 hours a week and making very little money, then the same applies. What went wrong with your business plan?

But let's assume that after six months or so things are ticking over nicely, work is beginning to take on a pattern and the anxiety-linked dreams have eased back to a manageable one or two a month. Now is the time to sit back and take stock.

WORK/LIFE BALANCE

This is really what it's all about. There's little point in living in a beautiful rural area if you're working 18 hours a day and never get to see it. When you first become self-employed, it's incredibly difficult to turn down work. There's the fear that you'll never be asked by anybody ever again. This worry is particularly common among people who went through lean times in the early days of their business or came from an employed background.

So you need to come up with a system or set of rules to cap your hours in order to spend time with your family and to enjoy the countryside around you – which, after all, is the whole point behind this.

If you:

◆ run a shop (deli, florist, wine merchant)
◆ offer any sort of office-based skill (IT, desk-top publishing)
◆ or do anything which means being on the end of a phone to other businesses (environmental consultant, green campaigner/lobbyist)

then it's easier to set your hours because you have to stick largely to the conventional working day, with perhaps an extra hour or two morning and evening to first prepare and then wrap up afterwards.

Other trades and skills will be more in demand in the evenings when potential customers and clients have returned home. This could apply to anyone offering private music tuition, portrait photography or home natural therapy treatments such as aromatherapy or reflexology. Other jobs may be decided by how many daylight hours there are. Landscape gardeners, thatchers or even dog walkers may not be as busy during the short winter days as they will be in the summer.

But for plenty of other jobs there's no outside factor and it's down to you to organise your time efficiently. There's not really an easy answer and everyone works differently anyway. But some of the options to consider are:

- Work a maximum of 10 or 12 hours a day.
- Always stop work in time to put the children to bed.
- Never work on a Sunday.
- Never work at weekends.
- Always take time to have lunch with your partner.
- Never take business calls before 8am on weekdays.
- Never take business calls after 8pm on weekdays.
- Never take business calls at weekends.
- Never respond to emails after 9pm at night, Monday to Saturday.
- Never respond to emails on a Sunday.

And so on. Each family works differently, so it's up to you to come up with a package that everyone's happy with. Then you have to stick to it.

HEALTH INSURANCE AND CRITICAL ILLNESS COVER

If you run your business alone and you're the main breadwinner in your family then some sort of medical insurance is vital. There's no company sick pay to fall back on when you are self-employed. Something as minor as a sprained ankle stops you driving for a couple of weeks. Even a bout of flu can keep you in bed for a few days. Then there are the more serious illnesses and accidents. Premiums will depend on your age, cover and lifestyle. Decent cover isn't cheap: you get what you pay for. But you have to ask yourself what would happen if you were unable to work, even for a short period.

CUSTOMER CARE

Your customers are your life blood. Nurture them, treasure them, care for them as carefully as you would your own child. So why is it that a ridiculous number of organisations still treat their customers as if they're getting in the way, an irritation to be swatted aside as quickly as possible? Large companies can get away with this sort of thing because there are plenty more customers where you came from, but small businesses can't. So follow the basic rules:

- Be nice to people, even if you've done a 16-hour day, it's raining, you have a headache and the previous ten customers have all been foul.
- Don't leave people waiting.
- Answer phones promptly.
- Return calls promptly.
- Answer correspondence promptly.
- If asked, give advice generously.
- Treat all customers in exactly the same way, regardless of their appearance or accent.

And be prepared to lose a sale if it means you gain extra goodwill. If your product or service isn't right for your customer, then say so. Offer them an alternative or suggest somewhere else they can go. Your honesty will earn you brownie points. You need to win the trust of your customer or client so they'll return and will also recommend you to others.

CASE STUDY: THE SNOWDONIA HOTELIERS

The family-run Buckley Pines Hotel is at the southern end of the Snowdonia National Park near the ancient market town of Machynlleth. Liz and Garry Wilson took it on in 1999, slowly renovating the building, which was purpose built as a five star hotel by a Victorian MP, Sir Edmund Buckley. These days it's a luxurious country house hotel with six en-suite letting bedrooms, all with stunning mountain views, a bistro, restaurant and bar.

Why a hotel?

Years ago we'd both worked in a hotel and had really enjoyed it. While the children were growing up, Garry managed a hosiery manufacturers. After they left school we seized the chance.

How prepared were you?

We drew a lot on Garry's previous managment experience. We spent time putting together a detailed business plan which we took to the bank. And we'd done our homework.

What was your biggest shock?

We were naïve about finding staff. If we didn't have the family, we couldn't have done it. Our son Damian does the bar, and our daughter Chantelle and I do the cheffing. We have a cleaner, and part-time waiting staff at weekends. Garry looks after the management.

Anything you would have done differently?

When we bought the hotel it was very rundown. We refurbished gradually while staying open. Looking back we would have been better off closing for six months and doing everything at once.

What tips would you pass on?

You have to have focus and your own goals. Listen to all the advice but at the end of the day you have to make up your own mind and stick to it. You need strong teamwork and total commitment. If one partner isn't as keen, then it isn't going to work.

Buckley Pines Hotel
Website: www.stayinwales.co.uk
Email: buckleypinehotel@aol.com
Tel/fax: 01650 531261

CUSTOMER FEEDBACK

Feedback from customers is a continual process and not something you only think about when you're starting up. Nothing is ever constant, and you, your business and your product or service should be constantly evolving. And how are you going to know what your customers think and want unless you ask them?

Feedback can be as complicated or as simple as you want to make it. If you have any contact at all with your customers then you're going to get some anyway, whether you like it or not. Listen carefully to what they have to say. Don't throw away your whole range and start again on the basis of one casual comment, but if a trend does begin to emerge then you have to react.

Aspects to get feedback on:

◆ **Price**. Are people saying your goods or services are too expensive, too cheap, good or bad value for money?

◆ **Range**. Are you offering enough variety for your customers or clients? Do you provide a wide variety of cheeses in your farm shop, can you as a furniture maker turn your hand to everything from a baby's highchair to a chaise longue or wardrobe?

◆ **Choice**. Do you offer enough choice of colours, sizes, woods, fabrics, ingredients, designs?

◆ **Special offers**. Do your customers or clients like special offers and respond to them? Should you be offering more or different special offers?

◆ **Speed of delivery**. Do your customers or clients complain about being kept waiting?

- **Availability**. Or are they irritated that the items you advertise, include on your website or list in a catalogue are 'out of stock'?

- **Quality of work or product**. Are your customers reporting back that your product is falling apart after a week? If you're a service provider, do you ever have to return to redo something?

- **Durability**. Has your product or service lasted as long as it should have?

- **Living up to expectations**. Does it do what it says on the tin?

- **General happiness**. Do most of your clients on the whole seem satisfied or disgruntled?

Feedback questionnaires

A lot of feedback will come at the point of sale. Regular and returning customers can tell you what they think next time they come in, but you have a problem if a first-time customer isn't happy and just doesn't return. That means they're going to grumble to whoever's around to listen and you'll have no chance to put things right.

So think about whether it's worth providing a more formal feedback system. Should you be sending out questionnaires a week or two after the sale? If so, make it easy for the customer or client to respond. Don't just write to them inviting their comments: no one will be bothered to write a letter back (except the angry, the bored or the pedantic). Instead, prepare a multiple choice questionnaire based on the above bullet points – price, range, choice and so on – plus other categories relevant to you. Then either ask for a grading for each section, points out of five for example, or ask the customer or client to tick a box – very satisfied, satisfied, adequate, poor and very poor. And leave a blank box at the bottom if they want to add any comments. Offer them anonymity if you think you may get more worthwhile feedback, though on the whole it's probably better if you know their names and addresses, especially if a serious problem does emerge.

You could also conduct the same sort of feedback survey over the phone, using the same questions as a basis for your interview, if you have customers' numbers, or by email.

Offer an inducement or bribe to encourage more customers to fill in the feedback questionnaires. It could be money off their next purchase, entry in a draw to win a case of wine, a year's free tree felling, whatever.

Any customer survey has to be proportionate to the value of your business. If you're selling holidays or bespoke furniture it probably is worth doing: if you're selling socks then it isn't.

Remote selling and feedback
If you only sell through an agent, shop or other third party, you'll never meet your customers. So think about whether you want to include brief questionnaires in the box or packaging of your product which will give the customers chance to respond directly to you. Make sure the label on the product gives your business name and a contact, either a website or email address or phone number.

You'll get a different sort of feedback from your agent or other third party which will be valuable, especially if they have plenty of experience in your field. But their interests won't necessarily be the same as yours, especially if they work on commission, dependent on volume of sales (you may prefer to concentrate on quality).

Suppliers and feedback

Depending on your business, it may also be worthwhile asking for feedback from suppliers. You're a novice and just starting out whereas they've probably been in the business for a long time and have seen everything. So ask them how they think you're doing: this will be easier if you've had a chance to build up a relationship with them first. It's in their best interests that you succeed because it's more business for them, so don't be shy about asking.

Staff feedback

If you employ staff then ask for their feedback too. This is even more important because they're often the first point of contact with the customer or client, by serving them in a shop, delivering to them, replying to their emails or answering the phone. Often a customer will be more open with an assistant than with the boss because it's less personal. Good staff will be invaluable in gathering customer feedback and reporting back to you.

CUSTOMER COMPLAINTS

From day one you need a policy on complaints. Obviously you need to observe a customer's statutory rights, but think about what your position is going to be above and beyond that. Even the best trader with the perfect product or service will get the odd complaint and it's far better to be prepared. That way, you'll sound confident and on top of the situation and will be able to maintain the initiative. Start waffling and you'll end up making sweeping concessions that you'll later regret.

Think about the following points and decide what your own policy is going to be:

- Is the customer always right?
- Would you ever make an exception?
- When?
- Is it better always to give them the benefit of the doubt?
- What are you going to do if a disgruntled customer starts shouting or becomes aggressive?
- How will you cope if it's in front of other customers or clients?
- What about customers who demand refunds?

As a general rule it is usually better to give customers the benefit of the doubt unless they're blatantly lying. Either way, let them get their complaint off their chest. Don't interrupt and listen carefully to what they have to say. When you do finally get to speak, respond to what they said rather than coming back at them with a prepared speech because this is far more likely to resolve things. If your unhappy customer makes a fuss in front of other customers, try to steer them into an office and away from the crowd. If that's not possible, then listen with patience and sympathy, and at the very least you'll escape with your dignity.

If the customer has a genuine grievance, then refund them their money with good grace. If the customer is probably wrong but is acting in good faith, then give them the refund anyway because it's good PR. But if the customer is 100 per cent wrong and even fraudulent (claiming money back on goods you're confident were shoplifted), then it's important to stand your ground.

SECURITY AND SHOPLIFTING

This isn't the inner city: steel shutters, security grilles and panic buttons are not going to be needed. But if you have premises there are still some basic precautions to take.

There are two types of shoplifters: professional thieves who make their living from it and opportunistic amateurs. Professionals target larger shops and concentrate on times when staff numbers are low, at lunchtime or towards the end of the day. They also pick times when staff concentration isn't going to be at its peak, either at the beginning of the day when people are greeting each other and talking about what was on TV the night before, or just as the store's closing when everyone's preparing to go home. Amateurs tend to pick times when the shop is busy and seize their chance.

Thieves and shoplifters look like anybody else, but be wary of anyone:

◆ wearing a coat or a thick woolie when it's warm outside
◆ with a coat or jacket draped over their arm
◆ with a large bag
◆ who seems nervous or who doesn't make eye contact
◆ who keeps looking around
◆ who browses without seeming to see
◆ with a shopping trolley or baby buggy with plenty of concealed shelves and spaces, and doing one of the above.

How to keep shoplifting and fraud to a minimum
◆ At the design stage of your shop or studio make sure there are no dark or concealed corners.

◆ Have well-lit large shelves with stock neatly displayed. This doesn't mean everything has to be in geometric lines, just make sure there is a sense of order so that any gaps are immediately obvious.

◆ Don't put small, valuable and easily grabbed items by the door.

◆ Keep anything exceptionally valuable behind the counter.

- Never turn your back on an open till.

- Keep a minimum of cash in the till.

- Be suspicious of high value notes, especially if they're used to buy cheap items.

- Be suspicious of any item that seems too cheap. Has someone switched price tags?

- Be suspicious of anyone who tries to distract or hurry you at the till.

Always acknowledge customers: it's polite and good practice anyway. If you're suspicious of anyone, then walk past them or make them aware that you're keeping a discreet eye on them. But always put personal safety first. If you think there may be a confrontation or if you feel threatened, get back behind the counter. Don't stand between them and the door. If they run off, don't follow them. Call the police.

Robberies

If you are unfortunate enough to be the victim of a robbery give them what they want. Don't make sudden movements, don't stare, try to avoid eye contact and try to stay calm. Remember as much as you can about their appearance and voice.

CCTV

If you decide it's necessary to install CCTV, then be aware of the provisions of the Data Protection Act. The main point to remember is that the cameras can't be hidden: customers and any staff must be made aware that cameras are being used.

CHASING UP THE MONEY

Many businesses will be paid at the point of sale, but plenty of others (organic veg box suppliers, contract gardeners, child care providers) send out monthly accounts to customers and so are effectively giving credit.

One or two slow payers or bad debts can bring down a small business, especially if the cashflow is a bit lacking sometimes. The secret is making sure the debts don't mount up until it's too late to do anything. Keeping accurate and up-to-date books allows you to spot early on any potential problems or consistently late payers.

Getting paid on time

Many small businesses report that the best way to get late payers to settle is to pursue them gently but persistently. Email, write or phone when you say you will and keep doing it. Don't let matters drift because your customer will relax and the momentum will be lost.

You're allowed by law to charge late-payers extra. You can charge interest on the overdue amount once the credit period has passed. Unless terms and conditions state otherwise, it's usually 30 days. If you try charging interest, it's usually calculated daily at the Bank of England base rate, plus a percentage. It's also possible to claim compensation for unpaid debts. Speak to your accountant or business adviser in advance about the best policy for your business.

If you're squeamish or soft about ruthlessly chasing slow payers, especially if you know they may be in trouble themselves, perhaps because of another unpaid bill, then remind yourself that you in turn will get pursued if you can't settle your debts on time.

Bad debts

Chasing debts yourself by going to court and filling in the court forms is not that hard: the staff there are generally helpful, particularly if it's a small claim. But you still need to ask yourself:

◆ Is the debt worth it?

◆ What are your chances of winning?

◆ Even if you do win, does the other side have the money to pay? If they have no cash or assets then the court can't force them to pay.

◆ Do you have the spare cash to cover your legal fees and other expenses while making the claim? (You may have insurance cover for this.) If you win you should get back some of your costs, but not necessarily all.

If you're owed a large sum of money, speak to your solicitor or accountant about the best way forward.

14

The Money
Part 2: After You Start Trading

B y now, hopefully, the money should have started to flow in. And if
you haven't realised already, this is the point when you'll discover
if you're any good at handling it.

A lot of it is down to being positive, confident and organised, and
the willingness to put in a few hours thinking about it. You should
be strongly motivated: after all, it's your money and your future
that it affects. So why not at least try and you may even surprise
yourself, though there'll always be a minority who get figure
blindness and break out in a sweat at the first mention of a balance
sheet. In that case find an accountant you can trust and leave it to
them.

But stuffing cash under the bed or in a box of onions isn't an option because:

- It'll get lost.
- It'll get stolen.
- The mice will eat it.
- Inflation will erode its value.
- You won't use it to reinvest in the business to make it healthy and strong.
- The Inland Revenue will get you in the end anyway.

It's all about managing the money side of your business as painlessly as possible, finding a way that suits you and then sticking to it.

TAX

If you're a sole trader or a member of a partnership you'll probably be self-employed and will pay income tax on that basis. If you've set up a limited company then you're an employee and will pay income tax on the salary you draw, while the company will pay corporation tax on any profits (defined as sales income less business expenses).

There's no definitive test for deciding if you're self-employed, but the usual criteria include:

- You mostly control your own working conditions (how many hours you do, what you do and where).
- You're free to hire other people to do work you've taken on.
- You've risked your own money in the business.

The two different systems

It's important to establish your status (self-employed or employee) because it will affect how the income tax is calculated, how much you'll pay and when you pay it.

If you're self-employed:

- You'll be taxed on your business's profits after any allowable expenses have been deducted (see below).
- You'll be responsible for paying your own tax.
- You'll be responsible for paying your own National Insurance.
- You (or your accountant) will have to complete an annual tax return.
- You'll pay tax twice a year, in equal instalments in January and July. The figures will be based on your previous year's tax bill.

If you're an cmployee:

- You'll pay income tax at the usual rates on the salary you draw from the business (2004/05: there are bands of 10, 22 and 40 per cent on earned income above your personal allowance. The higher rate cuts in at more than £31,400 pa).

- You'll also be taxed on any dividends or benefits you receive from the company, any return on your investment, and on any loan the company may make to you.

- You may not have to fill in a tax return.

- You'll pay income tax and NI monthly through your pay, or weekly if you're paid weekly.

It is possible to fall into both camps if you're employed some of the time and also carry out freelance work. Gardeners, for example, may work for a nursery or horticultural supplier while at the same time having their own private clients. If this applies to you, speak to your accountant about the simplest way to structure things.

NATIONAL INSURANCE

The type and amount of National Insurance you pay is also decided by whether you're self-employed or an employee.

If you're self-employed:

◆ You have to pay Class 2 contributions (2004/05: £2.05 pw).
◆ You also have to pay Class 4 contributions (2004/05: 8 per cent of your annual profit between £4,745 and £31,720, and 1 per cent on profits above that.

If you're an employee:

◆ You have to pay *employee's* Class 1 contributions. This is called PAYE, or Pay As You Earn (2004/05: 11 per cent of weekly earnings between £91–£610, and 1 per cent on earnings above that).

◆ Your business has to pay *employer's* Class 1 contributions for you and any other employee (2004/05: 12.8 per cent of employee's weekly earnings above £91 pw).

There's no argument when it comes to NI. By law, anyone in business has to pay it. The only exceptions are if your earnings or profits are below the small earnings exception limit or if you're over retirement age.

There's an Inland Revenue helpline to answer contributions queries from the newly self-employed. The number is 08459 15 45 15.

CORPORATION TAX

This depends on the size of the company and level of profits. The main rate is 30 per cent, but only on taxable profits above £1.5m a year. Below that, the rates increase gradually. If your taxable profits are less than £10,000 a year you won't pay any corporation tax at all.

VAT

You have to register for VAT if your business turns over more than a set amount each year. In the financial year 2005/06 the threshold was £60,000. It's usually increased by the government annually. If you're just starting out then £60,000 probably sounds like huge riches, but it's not. Remember that it's on turnover and not profit, so every penny passing through your business counts towards the total. Even a modest business can easily achieve that.

What makes it worse is that VAT applies in any period of 12 months, not just a fixed financial year. So that means that if your business turns over a penny more than the threshold in a single day at any time in the last year then you have to register for VAT. And you only have 30 days to do this from the end of the month in which your turnover goes over the threshold or you could be fined.

If you do have to register for VAT it's not a disaster, but it does mean you'll have more paperwork to do. If you think your turnover is hovering around the threshold, then consider trying to stagger the payments you receive over a longer period to keep yourself below the limit.

On the other hand it can be beneficial for businesses to register for VAT. In some cases you can register for VAT even if your business turnover is below the threshold – this is called voluntary registration. The main reason you may want to do this is because it means you can claim back VAT on your costs. But remember that you'll have to charge VAT on sales, and in order not to lose out you may have to increase prices which may make you uncompetitive. This may not matter to your customers if they're VAT registered because they, in turn, can claim it back.

There's also an argument which says that being VAT registered gives your business more credibility (makes it appear more grown-up).

CAPITAL GAINS TAX (CGT)

Because you're just starting out on your business life, selling assets is probably the last thing on your mind. But you should be aware that if and when you dispose of assets, if they're worth more than you paid for them, less various allowances, you may be liable for CGT. Premises are considered an asset. If you're self-employed you could be taxed personally, while limited companies pay corporation tax on any capital gains.

If you're really looking that far ahead then speak to your accountant. Otherwise don't even think about it for now, especially because the allowances and reliefs you can offset against any capital gains are relatively generous, and you'd have to make a thumping profit on any asset sale for it to really hurt.

IMPORT AND EXPORT

◆ If you're planning to sell goods to businesses outside the UK, you may not have to charge VAT on the sale. There are different rules for EU and non-EU countries.

◆ You have to pay duties on some imported goods.

If you fall into either of these categories, check the Customs and Excise website www.hmce.gov.uk or phone its national helpline on 0845 010 9000.

TAX RETURNS

Both the self-employed and directors of limited companies have to complete a tax return each year. The Inland Revenue will send you one every April, at the start of the financial year, and it should be tailored to your circumstances (though perhaps not in the first year). If you return the form by the end of September the Inland Revenue will work out your tax for you. If you decide to try and work out your own tax, or if your accountant does it for you, you have until the end of January to return the form or you can fill out and submit your tax return online, in which case it's calculated for you. But don't leave it until a few days before the deadline because that's when everyone else will be doing it too and you may have problems accessing the site.

If you've set up a limited company, then the company is responsible for calculating and paying tax on its profits. Its accounting period, usually 12 months, starts when the company is incorporated. It doesn't have to follow the financial year April to April but can be altered to suit your business, providing it's not extended by more than 18 months. Submitting accounts and making sure PAYE is set up correctly is complicated. Speak to your accountant if you're thinking about going down this route.

DOING YOUR BUSINESS EXPENSES

There are two types of business expense, running costs and capital allowances. It's important that they're separated out because while they both help reduce your eventual tax bill and therefore save you money, they do so in different ways.

Running costs

Allowable expenses include:

- costs of goods or materials bought as stock and then re-sold
- rent and running costs for premises
- general running expenses (postage and phone)
- financing costs (interest on loans)
- marketing costs (advertising, brochures, promotions)
- costs of travel to see customers
- work clothes, for example chef's protective aprons or children's entertainer's costume.

You're not allowed to include personal expenses, such as the costs of travelling to work or your own living expenses, or any bills for entertaining clients.

With running costs, you add up what you've spent in your financial year, deduct the total from what you've earned and pay tax on whatever is left.

If for any reason you've benefited personally from anything that you're including in your accounts as a running cost, then you can only claim a proportion of it. For example, if you run your furniture-making business from an annexe of your home but pay a single electricity bill, you can only claim the percentage of the bill that reflects how much power your business actually used.

Capital allowances

Capital allowances include:

- the cost of buying equipment
- the cost of buying premises, but only if they're agricultural or industrial.

In theory, a caterer's wooden spoon is equipment and therefore a capital allowance or item. In practice, though, capital allowances usually cover larger items. There's no Inland Revenue hard and fast rule, but anything costing more than about £70–£100 is usually considered a capital item.

So using the caterer as an example, their running costs would include eggs, flour and chocolate (in the category of goods bought as stock and then resold), while an allowable travel cost could be a journey to the wholesaler or to the farm shop which sells the finished product on their behalf. And a capital allowance could be the industrial oven or van used for deliveries, or the cost of buying a unit on a small trading estate which will be used as the kitchens.

The whole cost of the capital allowances can't be deducted from your gross income in the same way as running costs can be. Instead, each year you're allowed to claim a proportion of the value of the capital items. In the tax year 2004/05, small businesses could claim 50 per cent of the value of the capital item in the first year, and 25 per cent on the diminishing balance in subsequent years.

For example, our caterer buys a six-burner industrial oven for £1,600.

Year One

50 per cent of the cost to offset against income:	£800
Leaving a balance of:	£800

Year Two

25 per cent of the balance to offset against income:	£200
Leaving a balance of:	£600

Year Three
25 per cent of the balance to offset against income: £150
Leaving a balance of: £450

And so on. In this way, you maintain a pool of capital allowances to carry forward each year. In theory you can continue claiming 25 per cent on the diminishing balance for eternity. In practice, when it gets to a couple of pounds there's not much point. Instead what usually happens is that you buy a new capital item to replace the one that's worn out or broken, and the whole cycle starts over again.

A different rate applies for the purchase of industrial buildings. It's 4 per cent, both for the first year and subsequent years. In other words, in Year One you can offset 4 per cent of the cost of buying the building against your income. In Year Two, it's 4 per cent of the reduced total from the year before, and so on.

These rates do vary from time to time, and there are other rates for large companies, as well as different rates for other types of less common expense. In these cases, check the latest rules with your accountant or on the Inland Revenue website www.inlandrevenue.gov.uk.

PROFIT AND LOSS ACCOUNT

After having worked out your total expenses for the year (both running costs and capital expenditure) and your income, you can then use the figures to put together a profit and loss account. Don't let the name put you off: it just shows how much money you have made or lost in a financial year (which may or may not be the same as a calendar year). This can be as simple or as complicated as you want to make it: as long as it's clear and correct it doesn't really matter.

So, our caterer has been in business a couple of years and he's doing all right. There's plenty of room to grow but the business is at least in profit. The accounts could look like this.

Financial year: 2004/05

Income for year:	£20,000
Less running costs:	£4,000
Less capital allowances:	£6,500
Caterer pays tax on:	£9,500

(In practice, sales are usually broken down into categories, for example, cash sales, credit sales. Running costs would also be broken down into categories, as above, and entered accordingly.)

If our caterer makes a loss, this loss can be carried forward and used to help reduce his tax bill in future years. For example, if in Year Four he has a catastrophic few months – he breaks a leg and can't work and then the kitchens burn down – his income is dramatically reduced. Instead of being in profit, he makes a loss of £5,000.

In the profit and loss account for the next year, Year Five, that £5,000 is entered as a cost, in the same way as running costs and capital allowances are, and our caterer only pays tax on whatever is left.

BALANCE SHEET

Again, there's no deep mystery. A balance sheet simply shows where your business is, how much money it has and how much money it's owed, on the day or period you put the data together. It's really just a snapshot of your business at a given time.

It can be as simple or as labyrinthine as you want to make it. All sorts of things can get buried in balance sheets, but it's doubtful you'll need to get into that much creative detail so early in your business career.

Say you have a small landscape gardening and garden maintenance business. Your balance sheet could look like this.

Fixed assets:

Van	£5,000
Lawnmower	£1,000
Chainsaw/cutter	£600
Other equipment	£5,000
Total	£11,600

Current assets:

50 bags of compost	£200
16 tonnes of chippings	£150
Plant stock	£500
Cash	£1,000
Customers owe you	£3,500
Total	£5,350

Less current liabilities:

You owe to creditors	£2,500
Overdraft	£1,000
Equipment HP	£1,000
Total	£4,500

Working capital (current assets less liabilities)	£850
Your capital in the business	£12,450

HOW MUCH TO DO YOURSELF

Many people in business never go near a profit and loss account or a balance sheet and instead leave everything to their accountant. You should, however, at least know what they are so that you can:

◆ minimise your chances of looking like a complete idiot

◆ minimise your chances of being ripped off/blinded by figures until you find yourself an accountant you can trust

◆ enhance your business credibility, especially important if you're ever likely to need outside funding.

If you do decide to have a go at the book-keeping yourself then remember the Golden Rule: do it little and often. Every week is probably about right. Set aside a regular time. It could be in an evening after the children have gone to bed, or perhaps sometime during the working day when you know from experience that things are likely to be less busy.

If your business is small and well-organised, it shouldn't take much longer than an hour or two to sort through receipts, list what sales you've made and debts that are still outstanding. But if you let things slip, it'll be quickly become an ogre. And the worse it gets, the less likely you are to do something about it.

KEEPING RECORDS

The trick to running an organised business that makes the most of its opportunities, and minimises the risk of running out of stock or cash, is to keep good records. It sounds boring but unfortunately it's true. It helps you make sure you're meeting targets and should help you spot any problems before they become serious. It should also ensure that your spending is under control. Writing out cheques or authorising money transfers without any clear idea of your trading position is a one-way road to disaster.

There are also good reasons outside your business why you should keep proper records. Firstly, by law you must keep records of your business income and expenditure for at least six years after the latest date for sending back your tax return. And second, if your business ever faces a thorough audit by the tax inspectors, you need to be able to back up your claims with documentary proof.

15

Growing Your Business

A fter a year or two, when things have settled down and you've had chance to catch your breath, you'll find your priorities switching. Assuming it's no longer a question of day-to-day survival, you'll be looking around to see what needs changing or refining, how you'll find new customers, and how you'll increase your profits. Can you find new and better value suppliers of the dry items you use in your special occasion cakes? You've saturated the local area with your sales of stained glass windows, so what about the next county? Is it time to add a new seasonal line to your soft furnishings collection?

OVERTRADING
But while you think about expansion and growth, you also need to guard against hitting the small trader's 'wall'. This is where the

orders are flooding in too fast and there's too much work for one person, but you don't feel ready, either financially or emotionally, to expand. There's not a straight answer to this one. Clearly it makes no sense to take on staff until you feel the time is right: on the other hand it doesn't make any more sense to turn away business. If you're in this position, the choices include:

◆ Taking on a part-time employee for a handful of hours a week before committing yourself to someone full-time.

◆ Sub-contracting some of your orders out.

◆ Reducing your number of orders by raising prices.

◆ If appropriate, aiming for a longer delivery time.

◆ Looking carefully at your time management. Could you be working more efficiently?

There's no disgrace in staying small, and many make the deliberate choice to do so. Taking on staff involves much more paperwork and legal responsibility, and you may decide that rapid growth is not why you decided to become self-employed in the first place.

Whatever you decide, you need good, solid information to base your decision on: don't risk everything on a dodgy artistic instinct. So that means monitoring how much you're earning, calculating how much it's costing you to produce your goods or services, and then working out how much working capital you have available.

CASE STUDY: THE WEST COUNTRY HOLIDAY LETTING AGENCY

Tony and Clare Tregoning started Classic Cottages at their kitchen table in West Cornwall in 1977, marketing the four holiday cottages they'd bought with Tony's pay-off from leaving the army. Now they have 615 properties on their books, employ 25 people and turn over £7 million a year. Tony and Clare's son Simon, a former Bank of England banking supervisor, now runs the business.

What gave Tony and Clare the original idea?

Mum and dad had guessed that self-catering was going to be the next big thing. When they started marketing their own properties, other local owners asked them to take on theirs too. It dawned on them that there was a full-time business there, so they sold their own properties to finance it and the agency was born.

How did you grow the business?

It was a steady, organic growth rather than a big bang. We'd got to about 250 cottages by the mid 1980s. We'd expanded out of Cornwall and had taken on properties in Devon, Dorset and Somerset, and Cornish Cottages had become Classic Cottages. I joined the company in 1989 and we set ourselves a target of 500.

World domination now?

No, we'll stick to steady growth and the area we know – the West Country. There are no plans to grow by acquisition or mount a push to go nationwide.

What tips would you pass on?

Be ready to change your business model in the first year. What you first thought of may not be right, so be ready to adapt.

Anything you wish you'd done differently?

Sometimes we should have been more ruthless with staffing. It's a family business and we look after our staff, but it's bad for the business and unfair on the rest to be too soft on a member of staff who is not performing.

Classic Cottages
Website: www.classic.co.uk
Tel: 01326 555555

GOING INTO PROFIT

It could take months or even a year or two to go into profit. This isn't necessarily bad because in the early years you may decide that this isn't your priority. In many cases, building up a regular and loyal client base may be more important, especially if you're providing a service.

If for example you've set up a tailored walking holiday company appealing to the affluent empty-nesters, you'll need time to put together a customer list because the process of selling a holiday and it being taken can take months, unlike a pair of shoes or a pot where the customer buys it, takes it home and uses it half an hour later. You also need time to make the contacts for accommodation providers, transport providers and so on.

What you're doing is sacrificing profit in order to establish your client list, and gambling on reaping the benefits of repeat business in the later years.

HOW TO INCREASE SALES

You have three basic options:

- Sell more of the same thing to existing customers. Persuade them to take larger and more expensive organic veg boxes.

- Find new customers in the next county for your veg boxes.

- Sell different things to both old and new customers by diversifying into jams, chutneys and relishes.

Market research and customer feedback should show you the best way forward. Is there a demand for larger veg boxes? How many customers would pay for a special 'premium' selection? Is it cost-effective to send your boxes into the next county? Would it be more profitable to find a single distributor who could take on the boxing and local distribution himself? Are customers telling you they'd like the chance to buy local and homemade chutneys and relishes? If so, how much more would they be prepared to pay over and above what supermarkets charge? Is the presentation of the jar important to them? And so on.

These three basic options on increasing sales can be applied to virtually any type of business.

WHY YOU WANT CASH RESERVES

As your business grows, then hopefully so will your profit. With spare cash (!) you have three basic choices:

- Give yourself a pay rise.
- Keep it in reserve.
- Invest in new equipment and in developing the business.

If you were the sort of child who was encouraged to have a savings habit, then you probably still have it. Unfortunately in business that's not always a good thing. So keep some money in reserve for contingencies and emergencies, but don't overdo it.

There are sound reasons why it's probably more tax-effective to invest in new capital items. The money will also work harder for you if you're using it to grow your business and maximise your potential. And in times of low inflation then money sitting in the bank is virtually depreciating anyway.

So think carefully about your level of reserves. And remember that if you do need money in a hurry then you can borrow. Borrowing in business is perfectly acceptable as long as it's controlled and deliberate, and not a final desperate measure.

WHY YOU NEED (SOME) STOCK RESERVES

It's not wise to hold too much stock. It means that:

+ Too much cash is tied up.
+ You need somewhere to keep it all.
+ It may deteriorate.
+ It may go out of fashion.
+ It may become obsolete.
+ Customer demand may change.
+ You'll lose business flexibility.

This final point is critical. You run an accessories shop and see an obvious swing in demand looming, away from the wintery velvet handbags to this spring's new and shorter sarongs. But you overbought on the winter bags. Boxes of them are piled up out the back. What do you do? Sell them off cheaply to try and recoup some of the money to spend on the new sarongs? Borrow to pay for the new line and hope you can shift the bags at full price next winter? (But by then they'll be dated.) Is there room for the boxes of sarongs on top of the boxes of bags? Who knows? But if you hadn't overbought on stock in the first place then you wouldn't have this problem.

The trick is to find suppliers who can supply relatively small quantities at short notice.

COUNTING YOUR CHICKENS

You may not have realised it because you were too busy running a business, but by now you've probably built up quite a good range of skills. You're probably a:

- communicator
- planner
- sales person
- negotiator
- book-keeper
- IT trouble shooter
- administrator
- advertising manager.

As your business starts to grow, take time to assess your strengths and weaknesses. You've picked up all these new skills but you'll be better at some than others, and you'll also enjoy some aspects more than others. A surprising number of small traders report that they secretly enjoy the bookwork. Assuming there are no terrible disasters to unearth, it can be a calming and repetitive occupation, and tangible proof that you actually did start your own business and have found real, live customers.

But perhaps your assessment of your skills has shown that selling is your weak point, and you don't enjoy it anyway. Maybe you struggle with keeping your IT systems working. Or is it the donkey work involved in weighing and dry mixing your special occasion cakes that bores you to tears? If so, if money allows and you feel the time is right, think about employing someone to plug the gaps. Remember that you don't have to employ them directly. Use an agent who'll place your pottery or jams in the right shops, or find a freelance IT trouble shooter who'll come and sort out your systems quickly if they ever crash.

HOW TO BE THE BOSS

Directly employing staff brings with it a whole new set of responsibilities. A lot of it isn't negotiable because as an employer you have legal and regulatory obligations to your staff. Much will depend on your type of business, but the main points to be aware of include:

- health and safety
- income tax and National Insurance
- employment legislation to ensure equal rights (sex, race, disability)
- appropriate insurance cover.

But taking on staff goes beyond your legal and statutory obligations. You also have to think about:

- recruitment
- interviewing and appointments
- terms of employment including pay and hours
- areas of responsibility
- contracts
- training
- management of staff
- implications for your premises (is it big enough, sufficient loos, parking?).

Once you've got your staff, you can't leave them to it. Instead, because good and loyal long-serving staff can mean the difference between success and failure, think about how you're going to keep them. In the corporate world, staff turnover is usually considered a key indicator of the underlying health of the business. A high turnover means that something's going wrong somewhere and the problem needs to be addressed. It's far better if you don't get into that position in the first place. So:

- **Recruit carefully**. Spend as much time as you need to find the right person. Don't be blinded by academic qualifications: experience and enthusiasm can be more valuable.

- **Provide training** to enable them to do their job.

- **Provide a career path** by setting goals. More responsibility means more reward.

- **Recognise achievement** and acknowledge it.

- **Make them feel wanted and valued.**

- **Provide regular and constructive feedback.**

- **Listen to their opinions**, especially if they're in direct contact with customers when you may not be.

- **Create a good working environment**. Is it warm and comfy? Are the loos nice? Are there tea and coffee making facilities? A fridge? Fresh milk? Music?

In all these areas it's best to have your policy worked out in advance rather than making it up as you go along. Being reactive rather than proactive can lead to crisis management which is never a good idea. It's not going to be easy to come up with a foolproof system of management when you've never done it before, so if at all possible take advice from an experienced mentor or business adviser.

KEY DRIVERS, OR HOW YOU KNOW YOU'RE ON TRACK

You need to understand and monitor the 'key drivers' of your business. This is jargon for something that has a major impact on your business. It's helpful if you know the words because they crop up frequently, either from business advisers or in business literature. If you're looking to borrow to expand you may be asked to identify your own key drivers, and it's best if you don't look totally blank. So a key driver for a tailored walking holiday company could be as simple as the state of the weather (fewer customers in bad summers).

Despite the irritating phrase, key drivers are a good thing. They help you identify and focus on the really important aspects that you need in order to make your business a success. The walking holiday provider may not be able to do much about the weather, but he's aware that it's an issue therefore he may try to take more advance bookings which are less weather dependent or offer non-weather dependent alternatives (map reading lessons in a pub).

CASHFLOW

Successful businesses beginning to expand are particularly vulnerable to cashflow problems. The orders may now be flooding in for your bespoke garden furniture and you're working all hours to get everything done, but delivery time is eight weeks and you've allowed up to 30 days' credit on that, so you won't be seeing any money for three months. And in the meantime, because you've been working so hard on the making process, the paperwork has been neglected and you haven't had time to think about future marketing and sales.

This scenario shows how important it is to keep on top of the bookwork. Doing so will help you:

◆ Plan your workload over the year so you can use the quieter times to build up stock.

◆ Spot slow and non-payers and give you the chance to chase them up before it's too late.

◆ Make sure the cash flows smoothly through your business so that there's enough income to pay the bills at quieter times of the year.

Many businesses get around short-term cashflow problems by using their bank overdraft facility. That way you can pay your suppliers while you wait to be paid by your customers. Also, try to take a deposit when customers place their orders.

BORROWING

Overdrafts are known as short-term borrowing or finance. Loans are long-term borrowing. Small businesses usually use loans to buy larger items for their business because it's more cost effective, i.e. you usually pay less interest on a loan taken out and repayable over a fixed period than you do for an overdraft facility.

MORE VAT

Keep a careful watch on VAT. As a fledgling business you may not have breached the VAT threshold, but if you're expanding then you almost certainly will at some stage. You only have a limited time to register once your turnover exceeds that amount. VAT is explained in more detail in Chapter 14.

STRIKING THE BALANCE

There's a thin dividing line between achieving sustainable growth, which means not borrowing too much too fast, and holding your business back because you're nervous about getting in too deep. At this point, unless you're absolutely sure about which way to jump, go and talk to an expert you can trust and whose opinions you respect. It has to be someone who knows your business inside out, so it's probably going to be your accountant, bank manager or business adviser. Another pair of ears is always useful anyway.

They should help you review the financial health of your business, your tax situation and how you manage your affairs. They should also look at how to develop future marketing strategies and opportunities.

It's also useful to talk to a third party because they should be watching the wider picture that you've missed because you've been too busy working on your business. Is a savage interest rate rise looming which would cut people's income and therefore reduce the demand for your luxury product or service? Is health and safety legislation being tightened which may dramatically change how you operate your outdoor activities company? Or, closer to home, is a large new supermarket opening nearby which could severely dent the demand for your organic loaves?

The wider picture has just as much effect on your business as the situation in its own micro-climate. And it'll help you strike that balance which means the difference between success and failure for you.

THE END GAME

Running your own business is about personal satisfaction, fulfilling your own goals and, hopefully, living the dream. You only get one life, and nothing is sadder than someone who reaches the end and thinks 'if only...'.

That great entrepreneurial country, America, has generally a far more positive approach to business start-ups than the UK. There, it's far better to have tried and failed then never to have tried at all. And the stigma attached to business failure and even bankruptcy is much less than here. There have been valiant attempts in the last few years to dispel that stigma here, but it still lingers, even with an honourable failure (your two biggest debtors crash, taking you with them).

But go on, at least try, or you may spend the rest of your life regretting it. Don't be foolhardy and rush in without doing your homework. Live the dream, but at the same time don't forget your business head. Good luck!

Index